MEDICAL OFFICE TRANSCRIPTION

An Introduction to Medical Transcription

Karonne J. Becklin
Edith M. Sunnarborg

ABOUT THE AUTHORS

Karonne J. Becklin is the medical-secretarial program coordinator at Anoka-Hennepin Technical College in Anoka, Minnesota. In addition to her administrative responsibilities, she teaches courses in the medical-secretarial program, medical receptionist program, medical assistant program, medical transcription certificate program, and other administrative support career programs. Before her teaching experience, she worked as a hospital medical secretary. Mrs. Becklin is a Certified Medical Assistant, Administrative, and is a member of the AAMA and the AAMT.

Edith M. Sunnarborg, R.N., has a wealth of experience that includes hospital and clinic nursing, managing a medical office, and teaching in medical office career programs. Currently she is employed as a medical transcriptionist and a medical office consultant.

Medical consultant **Charles O. Gensmer**, M.D., Diplomate American Board of Internal Medicine—Pulmonary—graduated from the University of Minnesota. He did his postgraduate work at Shadyside Hospital in Pittsburgh and the University of Cincinnati, including a Pulmonary Fellowship at the University of Cincinnati. He is presently in practice at Midwest Internal Medicine.

This program has been prepared with the assistance of
Chestnut Hill Enterprises, Inc., Woodbury, Connecticut.

Send all inquires to:
Glencoe/McGraw-Hill
936 Eastwind Drive
Westerville, OH 43081

ISBN 0-02-802240-8

2 3 4 5 6 7 8 9   066   05 04 03 02 01 00 99 98 97

CONTENTS

PREFACE

The *Medical Office Transcription* program is designed for beginning medical transcription students. Many types of dictated medical documents, including chart notes, history and physical reports, consultations, office procedure notes, X-ray reports, progress notes, and letters are provided. The goals of the program are to develop transcribing speed and accuracy, gain skill in proofing and correcting documents, and increase student knowledge of medical terminology. Basic medical terminology, keyboarding, basic English skills, word processing basics, and general transcription are prerequisites to *Medical Office Transcription.*

◆ TO THE STUDENT

In using *Medical Office Transcription,* you will work with this text-workbook and the accompanying audiotape program. The program is divided into ten chapters. Chapter 1 is an introductory chapter; Chapters 2 through 10 each focus on an anatomical system of the body. These chapters begin with a short description about the anatomy and function of the system. Common structures are labeled on appropriate diagrams, and key words are given in italics. A section on clinical assessment explains observations made by the physician when evaluating a particular system.

The terminology section of each chapter contains medical words, terms that describe symptoms, and names of disease conditions with pronunciation of terms and brief definitions. These terms are used in corresponding chapter transcription. Some commonly performed procedures and laboratory tests are also listed and defined.

In addition, each chapter has (1) a list of medications with the pronunciation and classification of each drug, (2) a list of miscellaneous non-medical terms used in the chapter's dictated reports, (3) review worksheets to test your memory of the chapter's terms, and (4) hints for proper transcription.

The first part of each audiotape provides practice in word recognition and pronunciation. Listen and follow along in the text-workbook as each term is pronounced. You may wish to listen to the pronunciation a second time, so that you can practice spelling the terms. The second part of each audiotape contains the various reports and letters dictated for the chapter.

Each chapter of the text-workbook ends with a checkoff sheet, which serves as a record of your progress. Starting and completion dates of each item should be recorded, as well as the grade and/or number of errors.

The appendixes provide reference resources, drug classifications, a list of troublesome words, common abbreviations, and laboratory tests—information used when transcribing medical reports. Information provided by the American Association for Medical Transcription (AAMT) is also in the appendixes.

◆ ACKNOWLEDGMENTS

The following reviewers provided insight and guidance for which we are most grateful:

- ◆ Mildred S. Franceschi, Valencia Community College, Orlando, Florida

- ◆ Jan Krueger, Empire College, Santa Rosa, California

- ◆ J. Kevin Schmelzer, Southeastern Business College, Lancaster, Ohio

- ◆ Barbara Tietsort, Raymond Walters College/University of Cincinnati, Cincinnati, Ohio

INTRODUCTION TO MEDICAL TRANSCRIPTION

◆ INTRODUCTION

Medical Office Transcription provides you with the skills and knowledge necessary for beginning medical office transcription. Chapter 1 presents the goals of the program, the organization of this student text-workbook, the guidelines for preparing transcription in this program, and the preferred style for the documents being transcribed. Each of the subsequent chapters presents terminology and background information regarding one of nine systems of the body.

Course Goals

The following goals are addressed in this program:

Upon completion of the text-workbook and transcription, the student will be able to:

1. Apply written communication skills, including punctuation, capitalization, grammar, sentence structure, letter formats, report formats, and so forth.
2. Use designated references.
3. Review and apply medical terminology.
4. Maintain a medical word list.
5. Follow dictation instructions.
6. Apply basic medical transcription guidelines.
7. Develop speed during medical transcription.
8. Develop accuracy during medical transcription.
9. Transcribe and create appropriate medical documents.
10. Proofread and edit medical documents.

Chapter Sequence

The text-workbook chapters and dictation tapes are presented as follows:
1. Introduction to Medical Transcription (Tape 1)
2. The Integumentary System (Tape 2)
3. The Respiratory System (Tape 3)
4. The Cardiovascular System (Tape 4)
5. The Digestive System (Tape 5)

6. The Endocrine System (Tape 6)
7. The Urinary System (Tape 7)
8. The Reproductive System (Tape 8)
9. The Musculoskeletal System (Tape 9)
10. The Nervous System (Tape 10)

◆ BASIC MEDICAL TRANSCRIPTION GUIDELINES

Review and apply the following guidelines to your transcription:

1. Use commas in the following situations:
   a. Set off nonessential words and phrases.
      Dr. Jones, a first-year resident, is on call.
   b. Set off introductory subordinate clauses and introductory phrases.
      After the cast was applied, the X ray showed the fracture to be in good alignment.
      To check whether the fracture was in good alignment, an X ray was taken after the cast was applied.
   c. Separate the year from a complete date.
      The surgery is scheduled for Tuesday, May 1, 19--.
   d. Separate degrees, titles, and so forth, following names.
      The patient was referred to Phil Stevens, Ph.D., for psychological testing.
   e. Separate items in a series.
      The sponge, needle, and instrument counts were correct.
   f. Separate independent sentences connected with a conjunction.
      Mrs. Tina Roe called about an hour ago, and she still insists on seeing the doctor today.
      Note: Place commas and periods inside quotation marks.
      The patient states he feels "fuzzy in the head," and he needs medication for this symptom.
   g. Set off a direct address in a sentence.
      Set the chart on the desk, Janis, and take the new dictation tape with you.
   h. Separate equal adjectives (modifiers).
      The patient is a well-nourished, well-developed female.
   i. Indicate missing words.
      Chest X ray, normal. (Note: Chest X ray was normal.)
   j. Separate parts of an inverted diagnosis.
      Ankle sprain, left.

2. Use semicolons in the following situations:
   a. Separate independent clauses (sentences) without a conjunction.
      The surgery was scheduled for 4 p.m.; it lasted four hours.
      Note: Place semicolons outside quotation marks.
      The patient said, "I will obtain my medical records"; she did not bring them to the office.
   b. Set off independent clauses that already contain one or more commas and have a conjunction.
      If the appointment has been made, Janet can leave at 9:30 p.m.; or if the appointment has not been made, she needs to leave right away.

   c. Separate two independent clauses joined by a transitional expression such as *therefore, however,* and so forth.
The doctor will be two hours late; however, there are no patients scheduled until this afternoon.

   d. Separate items in a series when the items have commas.
The doctor has lectures scheduled in St. Paul, Minnesota; Fargo, North Dakota; and Des Moines, Iowa.
BP, 120/54; pulse, 80/minute; respirations, 16/minute; and temperature, 98.4.

3. Use a colon in the following situations:

   a. Introduce a series of items.
The patient complains of the following symptoms: dizziness, lightheadedness, and palpitations.

   b. Separate hours and minutes.
The surgery is scheduled for 12:30 p.m.

   c. Set off headings and subheadings in a medical document. (*Note:* capitalize the first word after a heading.)
REVIEW OF SYSTEMS: Negative.

   d. Introduce an example, a rule, or a principle.
We have only one choice: immediate surgery.

4. Use capital letters in the following situations:

   a. Emphasize allergies in full capital letters. (*Note*: An alternative method is to use boldface and to underline allergies.)
The patient is ALLERGIC TO PENICILLIN.
The patient is <u>allergic to penicillin</u>.

   b. Name specific departments in an institution, such as Admitting Office, Operating Suite C, Intensive Care Unit, and so forth.
The patient was sent to Recovery Room C at 9 a.m.

   c. Capitalize trade and brand names, but do not capitalize generic names:
Tylenol #3, pHisoHex, Cardizem, alcohol, catgut, aspirin

   d. Capitalize races, peoples, religions, and languages (Caucasian, Jewish, Hispanic, English, and so forth), but do not capitalize *white* and *black* when they refer to race.
The patient is a well-developed, well-nourished Caucasian male.
The patient is a well-developed, well-nourished black female.

   e. Use full capitalization for headings and subheadings.
GENITOURINARY: Exam will be completed next month.

5. Use a hyphen in the following situations:

   a. Separate the elements of compound adjectives that occur before a noun.
The patient has a low-grade temperature. (Note: The patient's temperature was low grade.)
This is a well-developed Asian male.

   b. Form "self" compounds.
The patient was self-employed.

   c. Consult a dictionary or other reference source for the proper spelling of nouns and adjectives as one word or with a hyphen.

follow-up
f/u

X ray (noun)

x-rayed (verb)

X-ray findings

The follow-up visit was scheduled for tomorrow.
Note: Verbs are generally spelled as two words, with no hyphens:
   The patient will follow up with hematology.

   d. Join a single letter to a word to form a coined compound word that is used as an adjective.
      The patient had a T-cell abnormality.
      The X-ray results will be available at the hospital.

6. Use abbreviations in the following situations:

   a. Use published abbreviations. Basic abbreviations for each system are presented in each chapter. The general rule is to abbreviate when the dictator abbreviates except abbreviate all measurements and pharmaceutical language.
      The mole is 1.25 cm in circumference with irregular borders.

   b. Use proper abbreviations to transcribe the times for the administration of medication. *Note:* Abbreviations for common prescriptions are provided in Appendix D.
      The patient was placed on Augmentin 125 mg TID x 5 days.
      A prescription for tetracycline 500 mg QID was given to the patient.
      Note: Always keep units of measurement on same line.

   c. Spell out an abbreviation if its meaning could be misunderstood.
      The patient has no history of a calcium problem.
      (For example, do not use CA, which can stand for *calcium, cancer, or coronary artery.*)

7. Use symbols when transcribing numbers or abbreviations. Some common examples are shown:

As heard:	As transcribed:
used two oh chromic catgut	used 2-0 *or* 00 chromic catgut
two by point five millimeters	2.0 x 0.5 mm
number two oh silk	#2-0 silk *or* No. 2/0 silk
one point two percent	1.2%
Pulses are two plus.	Pulses are 2+.
blood pressure one hundred twenty over eighty	Blood pressure: 120/80. *or* Blood pressure, 120/80. *or* BP: 120/80.
fifty-five milligrams percent	55 mg%
diluted one to one hundred	diluted 1:100
ninety-nine degrees Fahrenheit	99°F
at a minus two station	at a -2 station
medication times three days	medication x 3 days
one hundred milligrams per hour	100 mg/hr
normal "es" one and "es" two	normal S_1 and S_2 *or* S1 and S2 *or* S-1 and S-2
one hundred milligrams per teaspoon	100 mg/teaspoon

8. Use numbers as follows:

   a. Do not start a sentence with a number, such as "24-gauge needle was used."

A 24-gauge needle was used.

b. Always use Arabic numbers with technical measurements (except at the beginning of a sentence).
A #14 Foley catheter was inserted.

c. Express numbers in figures (including 1 through 10) when used as significant statistics such as age or as technical measurements.
The patient was given 10 tablets.
No. 10 tablets were given.
The patient was prescribed Paxil 20 mg QD, #60.

d. Spell out ordinal numbers and single fractions.
The patient was discharged on the fifth postoperative day.
The patient was placed on Amoxicillin 250 mg/5 ml, one-half teaspoon TID.

e. Use roman numerals in cranial nerves, EKG leads, EEG leads, and non-counting listings.
The exam found that the cranial nerves II-XII were intact.
The patient had Stage II carcinoma.

f. Spell out time on the hour when a.m., p.m., or o'clock is not used.
The patient will be seen at three.

g. Insert a zero in front of the decimal point that is less than a whole number.
The patient's prescription was changed to 0.125 mg.

h. Enumerate listings as much as possible.
DIAGNOSES: 1. *Right otitis media.*
2. *Laryngitis.*
3. *Pharyngitis.*
The diagnoses were (1) right otitis media, (2) laryngitis, and (3) pharyngitis.

9. Follow proper guidelines for letters and memorandums. Use a reference manual.

10. Utilize a reference manual for any questionable punctuation, capitalization, or grammar.

11. Use an acceptable, approved format for each medical document. Do *not* change heading styles within the document.

◆ TRANSCRIBING EXERCISES

The medical reports for this text-workbook pertain to dictation that would be given in a clinic or doctor's office. The types of reports include chart notes, progress notes, history and physical reports, X-ray reports, procedure notes, and consultations. (Refer to Appendix F, The Medical Record, for a review of the key parts of these documents.)

In a clinic the transcription may be keyed directly onto an 8½ by 11-inch sheet of paper, continuing from visit to visit with about one-half inch space between reports. Another method is to use shingles, which are individual paper forms that are keyed onto and then inserted separately into the patient's chart.

Each facility has its own format for transcribing doctors' dictation. One of the most common formats is the SOAP method, which has four essential components:

S: Subjective findings—what the patient tells the physician about the problem or complaint.

O: Objective findings—what the physician finds upon examination; it may include laboratory, X rays, and other diagnostic procedures.

A: Assessment—the diagnosis/diagnoses based on the above findings.

P: Plan—a course of treatment, such as further laboratory or X-ray studies, surgery, medications, referral, and so forth.

The facility may have a preference for complete headings or just the letters when working in the SOAP format.

Each entry in a chart should end with a signature line. This sign-off varies according to the policy of the clinic or doctor. The physician's or dictator's name may be followed by the initials of the transcriptionist at the center on the third or fourth line below the last entry line. The signature line may also include the date of dictation and transcription.

Debra Litman, M.D./kb
Lee W. Kim, M.D./kb D: 10/20/— T: 10/21/—

In this text-workbook, as a transcriptionist, you are employed by the Wilcox Medical Center, 6210 Eagle Street, Denver, Colorado 80239-7145. The physicians are John Blackburn, M.D., family practice; Lee W. Kim, M.D., internal medicine; Debra Litman, M.D., family practice; and Lynn Solinski, M.D., internal medicine. The complete headings are used for the SOAP format.

◆ FORMATTING DICTATION

Document formats and dictation styles vary from office to office. A prevalent format is the blocked style. For this text-workbook's assignments, use this style in preparing each type of report. The blocked styles and layout to be used are shown on the following pages.

CHART NOTE *(centered, all caps, l- inch top margin)*

↓3

Jason A. Others ↓3   ∧ 3/21   04/02/98
                                                        5.5

HISTORY OF PRESENT ILLNESS: This afternoon the patient developed some burning sensation when urinat-↓1
ing, followed by pain and hematuria. There was no penile discharge. ↓2

PHYSICAL EXAMINATION: BP, 189/70; pulse, 95; temperature, 96.5°F.

(indent   **ABDOMEN**: Soft with slight discomfort to palpation in the hypogastric region. No CVA
½ inch) tenderness.

          SCROTUM AND PENIS: Appear normal without discharge.

LAB: Urinalysis shows brown color, cloudy, and ketones small. Specific gravity, 1.021. WBC, 50-75; RBC, packed;
moderate bacteria. Culture was sent to outside lab.

DIAGNOSIS: Cystitis.

TREATMENT: The patient is ALLERGIC TO SULFA. Therefore, Amoxicillin 250 mg TID x 10 days and Pyridium
one tablet TID #6 were prescribed. The patient is to force fluids to 2000 cc daily and is to call for culture results in
2 days. Scheduled follow-up in 10 days. ↓3-4

(Start at center)   Lee W. Kim, M.D./xx

                                              signature line

BLOCKED FORMAT

CHART NOTE

Jason A. Others   3/2/--

SUBJECTIVE: This afternoon the patient developed some burning sensation when urinating, followed by pain and hematuria. There was no penile discharge.

OBJECTIVE: BP, 189/70; pulse, 95; temperature, 96.5°F.

    ABDOMEN: Soft with slight discomfort to palpation in the hypogastric region. No CVA tenderness.

    SCROTUM AND PENIS: Appear normal without discharge.

LAB: Urinalysis shows brown color, cloudy, and ketones small. Specific gravity, 1.021. WBC, 50-75; RBC, packed; moderate bacteria. Culture was sent to outside lab.

ASSESSMENT: Cystitis.

PLAN: The patient is ALLERGIC TO SULFA. Therefore, Amoxicillin 250 mg TID x 10 days and Pyridium one tablet TID #6 were prescribed. The patient is to force fluids to 2000 cc daily and is to call for culture results in 2 days. Scheduled follow-up in 10 days.

        Lee W. Kim, M.D./xx D: 3/2/-- T: 3/2/--

BLOCKED SOAP

WILCOX MEDICAL CENTER
6210 Eagle Street, Denver, CO 80239-7145
303-555-1026   Fax: 303-555-9320

2"

March 21, 19--

↓4

National Handicap Housing, Inc.
1050 South Fillmore Street
Denver, CO 80209-6578 ↓2

Ladies and Gentlemen ↓2

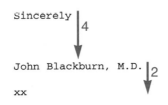

RE: ∧ Keith Atwood ∧   Patient #123-403 ↓2
    2#   tab

Mr. Atwood has been struggling with physical difficulties as well as with depression. During the time that I have seen him, he has been diligent in following up with appointments. His best period of sustained function occurred when he had a stable home life. During the past several months, he has had to make several residential moves. It is my opinion that this has exacerbated his condition both from physical and mental standpoints.

I would support any efforts to find permanent housing for him. Given his inability to work over the past several years, I believe that he would be a good candidate for low-income housing.

Please contact me if you have any additional concerns about Mr. Atwood's condition.

Sincerely

↓4

John Blackburn, M.D. ↓2

xx

LETTER EXAMPLE: Full block format, open punctuation (*Note:* The standard punctuation style has a colon after the salutation and a comma after the complimentary closing.)

X-RAY REPORT

12/03/98
~~12/3/~~

Kate Gonsinski

BILATERAL MAMMOGRAM: There is irregularly dense glandular tissue throughout both breasts. There are no suspicious masses or calcification seen. There is no radiographic evidence of malignancy. There has been no significant change compared with the previous study dated May 15, 19--.

CONCLUSION: Negative mammogram.

Karen Twan, M.D./xx   *signature line*

X-RAY REPORT: Block Format

PROCEDURE NOTE

Pamela W. Evanston   12/19/--

PROCEDURE: Colposcopy.

INDICATIONS FOR PROCEDURE: In October of this year, patient had a low-grade epithelial lesion of undetermined significance, probably mild dysplasia or CIN Grade I with HPV effect. For that reason, we scheduled her for colposcopy.

Patient is 21 years old, Para 1-0-0-1. Her age at first pregnancy was 19. She has no history of venereal disease or sexually transmitted infection.

PROCEDURE: After discussion of procedure, risks, benefits, and possible alternatives, patient gave written consent for the procedure.

Speculum was placed in the vagina and cervix brought into view. After applying vinegar, we saw a large transformation zone consisting of white epithelium with mosaic at 12 and 1 o'clock and punctation and mosaic at 5-6 o'clock. It was more extensive on the posterior cervix, but it went circumferentially and under the anterior cervix, possibly inside the os. Endocervical biopsies were done at 12 and 1 and at 5 and 6 o'clock. They were sent separately to Pathology.

DIAGNOSIS: Colposcopy for abnormal Pap smear.

PLAN: We will await pathology results of biopsies. Then we will recommend either cryocautery or loop electrosurgical excision procedure based on the severity of findings.

Les Perez, M.D./xx D: 12/19/-- T: 12/19/--

PROCEDURE NOTE: Block Format

◆   **REVIEW**

chart

Patient's name
Page 2
Date
JS

Letter

Addressee
Page 2
Date
JS

This part of the chapter first provides a review of anatomical combining forms and basic medical terminology. Then, several exercises are given for you to recall meanings of suffixes. In addition, there are exercises referring to the methods of examination, chart notes, body directional positions, common medical treatments, and classifications of medications.

ANATOMICAL COMBINING FORMS

Term	Meaning
adeno	gland
angio	vessel
arterio	artery
arthro	joint
blepharo	eyelid
cardio	heart
cephalo	head
cervico	neck
chole	gall
chondro	cartilage
costo	ribs
cranio	cranium, skull
cysto	bladder, sac
cyto	cell
dermo, dermato	skin
encephalo	brain
gastro	stomach
hemo, hemato	blood
hepato	liver
hystero, utero	uterus
leuko	white
lipo	fat
litho	stone
metro	uterine tissue
myelo	bone marrow, spinal cord
myo	muscle
nephro, reno	kidney
neuro	nerve
oophoro	ovary
ophthalmo	eye
osteo	bone
pharyngo	pharynx, throat
pneumono, pulmono	lungs
pyelo	pelvis of kidney
pyo	pus
rhino/naso	nasal tissue, nose
salpingo	fallopian tubes
spleno	spleen
thoraco	thorax, chest
thrombo	clot
uretero	ureter
urethro	urethra

GENERAL TERMS

The following terms are found generally throughout transcription. They apply to no particular system.

Practice word recognition and pronunciation; then spell each term. The macron (‾) is used for long vowels, and the breve (˘) is used for short vowels and for indefinite vowel sound of the schwa (ə). Stressed syllables are followed by a prime (′). A hyphen separates the remaining syllables. A review of medication abbreviations is incorporated throughout the transcription.

ache	(āk)	pain that persists
acute	(ă-kyūt′)	having a short and sharp course
adolescent	(ad-ō-les′ent)	person in teen years
afebrile	(ā-feb′ril)	not having an elevated body temperature
allergy	(al′er-jē)	sensitivity to a substance that results in symptoms
ambulate	(am′byū-lāt)	to walk about
anomaly	(ă-nom′ă-lē)	abnormality; deviation from normal
asepsis	(ă-sep′sis)	cleanliness
atrophy	(at′rō-fē)	wasting of a structure
benign	(bē-nīn′)	of mild character
breadth	(bredth)	width
calcification	(kal′si-fi-kā′shŭn)	deposit of lime or calcium salt
catheter	(kath′ĕ-ter)	tubular instrument that allows passage of air or fluid
chronic	(kron′ik)	marked by slow progress and long continuance
congenital	(kon-jen′i-tăl)	existing at birth
constriction	(kon-strik′shŭn)	tightening, squeezing, contraction, or narrowing
contaminate	(kon-tam′i-nāt)	to render unclean
contraindication	(kon-tră-in-di-kā′shŭn)	inadvisable
crisis	(krī′sis)	a sudden change
debris	(də′brē)	material that doesn't belong in an area; foreign
dehydration	(dē-hī-drā′shŭn)	reduction of water content
diaphoresis	(dī′ă-fō-rē′sis)	perspiration; sweating
dilate	(dī′lāt)	to widen
disease	(di-zēz′)	illness
disposition	(dis-pə-zish′ŭn)	treatment or management
distention	(dis-ten′shŭn)	the state of being stretched or enlarged
elicit	(i′lis-ĭt)	reveal; provide
etiology	(ē′tē-ol′ō-jē)	study of cause of disease
hypertrophy	(hī-per′trō-fē)	increase in organ size
immobile	(im-mō′bil)	not capable of moving
infection	(in-fek′shŭn)	invasion of area with pathogenic microorganisms
inflammation	(in-flă-mā′shŭn)	tissue reaction to injury (pain, warmth, swelling, redness)
injury	(in′jer-ē)	damage; trauma
malignant	(mă-lig′nănt)	harmful; causing death
manual	(man-yəl)	pertaining to the hand
metastasis	(mĕ-tas′tă-sis)	spread of disease to another body part
nausea	(naw′zē-ă)	feeling of having to vomit

necrosis	(nĕ-krō´sis)	dead, not viable tissue
obese	(ō-bēs´)	excessively fat
obstruction	(ob-strŭk´shŭn)	blockage
occlusion	(ŏ-klū´shŭn)	closed
postural	(pos´tyū-răl)	pertaining to position or posture
prognosis	(prog-nō´sis)	outcome
prophylaxis	(prō-fi-lak´sis)	something that prevents spread of disease
prosthesis	(pros-thē´sis)	artificial substitute for missing part
provisional	(prō-vizh´ə-nəl)	temporary
purulent	(pyūr´ŭ-lent)	containing pus
quadrant	(kwah´drant)	quarter of a section
radiate	(rā´dē-āt)	to spread
recur	(rē-kŭr´)	to happen again
regimen	(rej´i-men)	program or plan
retention	(rē-ten´shŭn)	keeping in; retaining
sensitivity	(sen-si-tiv´i-tē)	responding to
septic	(sep´tik)	not clean; contaminated
sibling	(sib´ling)	offspring of the same parents
specimen	(spes´ĭ-men)	sample
stat or STAT	(stat)	right now
stenosis	(ste-nō´sis)	narrowing
sterile	(ster´il)	free of all microorganisms and spores
stricture	(strik´chŭr)	narrowing of hollow structure
suture	(sū´chŭr)	noun: thread-like material, stitch; verb: to sew or stitch
symptom	(simp´tŏm)	sign
syndrome	(sin´drōm)	group of signs or symptoms
therapy	(ther´ă-pē)	treatment
tract	(trakt)	pathway
trauma	(traw´mă)	injury

TRANSCRIPTION CHECKOFF SHEET
by Patient

Worksheet 100
transcription
of practice

DOCTOR DICTATING:	John Blackburn, M.D.
TYPE OF DICTATION:	Chart notes, history and physical, X-ray report, and letters
DATE OF TRANSCRIPTION:	April 2, 19--

Item Number	Patient	Date Started	Date Completed	Grade/ Number of Errors
1	Carl Adams			
2	Cecelia Wert			
3	David Mendez			
4	David Mendez			
5	Letter to General Medicare RE: Mabel Ryerson			
6	Alison Beckman			
7	Michael Weysik			
8	Reis Olsson			
9	Letter to Laboratory Department, Wilson Hospital RE: Susan Yee Yang			
10	Letter to ABC Company, Inc. RE: Warren Thomas			

2 THE INTEGUMENTARY SYSTEM

◆ INTEGUMENTARY SYSTEM FUNCTION AND COMPONENTS

The skin, or *integument*, has the following functions:

◆ **PROTECTION:** As long as there are no breaks, the skin forms a protective barrier against infections and harmful substances. The skin also prevents excessive loss of water and salts.

◆ **ELIMINATION:** The skin helps remove some body wastes and water.

◆ **REGULATION AND INSULATION:** The skin helps to regulate the body's temperature through perspiration and through constriction and dilation of blood vessels, which help in the cooling process.

◆ **SENSATION:** The skin receptors are sensitive to pain, touch, temperature, and pressure.

As illustrated in Figure 2.1, skin consists of two layers of tissue: the outer (*epidermis*) and the inner (*dermis*). The epidermis is made up of epithelial tissue and contains the openings for the hair shafts and sebaceous (oil) glands.

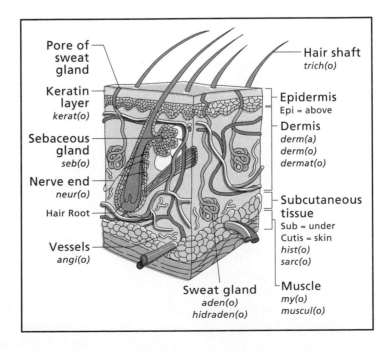

Figure 2.1 The Integumentary System

The dermis (cutaneous layer) contains hair follicles (roots), sebaceous glands, sweat glands, blood vessels, and nerve fibers. The area just below the cutaneous layer is called the subcutaneous layer and consists of fatty tissue.

◆ CLINICAL ASSESSMENT

The examiner observes skin for the following conditions:

◆ **COLOR:** normal, cyanotic, erythematous, flushed, jaundiced, pale

◆ **TEXTURE:** clammy, dry, moist, scaly

◆ **TURGOR:** elasticity

◆ **TEMPERATURE:** cold, warm

◆ **LESIONS:** any abnormalities

◆ SYMPTOMS AND DISEASE CONDITIONS

The following symptoms and disease conditions apply to the integumentary system.
   Practice word recognition and pronunciation; then spell each term.

abrasion	(ă-brā´zhun)	removal of superficial layers of skin
abscess	(ab´ses)	localized collection of pus
acne	(ak´nē)	inflammation of sebaceous glands
basal cell carcinoma	(bā´săl) (kar-si-nō´mă)	skin cancer
blister	(blis´ter)	fluid-filled structure under skin
boil	(boyl)	infection in hair follicle
cellulitis	(sel-yū-lī´tis)	inflammation of skin and subcutaneous tissue
comedos	(kom´ē-dōz)	blackheads caused by plugged oil gland
contusion	(kon-tū´shŭn)	bruise
cyst	(sist)	sac containing fluid
dermatitis	(der-mă-tī´tis)	general term indicating inflammation of skin
ecchymosis	(ek-i-mō´sis)	black and blue or purple discoloration of skin caused by bruise
eruption	(ē-rŭp´shŭn)	rash
erythema	(er-i-thē´mă)	reddish color to skin
excoriation	(eks-kō´rē-ā´shŭn)	break in skin caused by surface trauma; scratch
fissure	(fish´ŭr)	furrow; crack
fluctuant	(flŭk´tyū-ănt)	wavelike motion
herpes	(her´pēz)	viral disease characterized by eruption of vesicles on reddish bases
impetigo	(im-pe-tī´gō)	contagious superficial infection with vesicles and yellowish crusting
indurated	(in´dū-rāt-ed)	hardened or firm
keloid	(kē´loyd)	overgrowth of scar tissue
laceration	(las-er-ā´shŭn)	tearing of skin
lesion	(lē´zhŭn)	injury or pathological change in tissue
maculae	(mak´yū-lē)	colored spots on skin
nevus	(nē´vŭs)	circumscribed, pigmented (shade of brown) area of skin; mole

nodule	(nod´yūl)	knob, mass, or swelling
papule	(pap´yūl)	raised spot
paronychia	(par-ō-nik´ē-ă)	inflammation of nail fold
pediculosis	(pĕ-dik´yū-lō´sis)	infestation of lice
plantar wart	(plan´tăr)	wart on sole of foot, caused by a virus
pruritus	(prū-rī´tŭs)	itching
pustule	(pŭs´chūl)	pimple with pus
scabies	(skā´bēz)	eruption caused by mite that lays eggs in burrows under skin; characterized by intense itching
seborrhea	(seb-ō-rē´ă)	overproduction of oil from sebaceous glands, resulting in greasy skin
verruca	(vĕ-rū´kă)	overgrowth of dermis, caused by virus; wart
vesicle	(ves´i-kl)	circumscribed elevation of skin containing fluid

◆ SURGICAL PROCEDURES

| cryotherapy | (krī´ō-thār´ă-pē) | freezing the skin with liquid nitrogen |
| incision and drainage | | cutting into and leaving open for drainage |

◆ MEDICATIONS

acyclovir	(ă-sī´klō-vir)	antiviral
Ancef	(an´sef)	antibiotic
aspirin	(as´pi-rin)	analgesic; antipyretic
Bacitracin	(bas-i-trā´sin)	antibiotic
Betadine	(bā´tă-dīn)	antimicrobial
Coumadin	(kū´mă-din)	anticoagulant
E.E.S. (brand of erythromycin)		antibiotic
hydrocortisone	(hī-drō-kōr´ti-sōn)	corticosteroid
Iodoform	(ī-ōd´ō-form)	antimicrobial
Keflex	(kĕf´lĕx)	antibiotic
Kwell	(kwell)	scabicide
lidocaine	(lī´dō-kān)	anesthetic; antiarrhythmic
liquid nitrogen	(nī´trō-jen)	cryotherapeutic agent
Oxy-10	(oxē´ten)	keratolytic
Retin A	(ret´in-ā)	keratolytic
saline	(sā´lēn)	salt solution
Tetanus booster	(tet´ă-nŭs)	vaccine
Tylenol #3	(tī´len-ol)	analgesic
Xylocaine	(zī´lō-kān)	anesthetic

◆ MISCELLANEOUS TERMS

Ace bandage	(ās)	elastic bandage
copious	(kō´pē-us)	large amount
inflamed	(in-flāmd´)	characterized by pain, warmth, swelling, and redness

neonatal	(nē-ō-nā´tăl)	relating to a newborn child from birth to 28 days
prepped	(prept)	prepared
sterilely	(ster´il-lē)	in a manner that is free from living organisms
tinea	(tin´ē-ă)	fungal infection
Vicryl suture	(vī´kril)	type of suture material

TRANSCRIPTION CHECKOFF SHEET
by Patient

worksheet 96 transcription 93

DOCTOR DICTATING: John Blackburn, M.D.

TYPE OF DICTATION: Chart notes

DATE OF TRANSCRIPTION: April 5, 19--

Item Number	Patient	Date Started	Date Completed	Grade/ Number of Errors
1	Karen McMillan			
2	Patricia Smith-Wright			
3	David Bondham			
4	Ronald Glazier			
5	Lee Yang			
6	Elizabeth Norbak			
7	Summer Raintree			
8	Hank Rice			
9	Nancy Hurr			
10	Teresa Bixby			
11	Lucas Everson			
12	Janet Grossman			

THE RESPIRATORY SYSTEM

◆ RESPIRATORY SYSTEM FUNCTION AND COMPONENTS

Worksheet 100

The function of the respiratory system is to exchange oxygen from the air with carbon dioxide from the body cells. This process is known as *respiration*. A respiration refers to *inspiration*, or inhaling once (taking air into the system), and *expiration*, or exhaling once (letting air out of the system). A person's average respiratory rate is between 8 and 24 times per minute. Control of this rate is accomplished by factors that include a person's will, control by nerves or chemicals, and the use of the muscles between the ribs (intercostal muscles) and the muscle separating the thorax from the abdomen (diaphragm).

The breathing process is accomplished by the following organs (locate each organ in Figure 3.1).

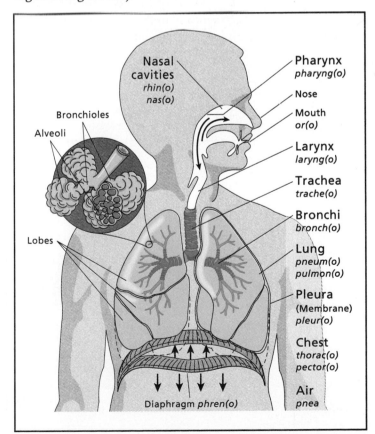

Figure 3.1 The Respiratory System

◆ **NOSE:** The nose is divided by a cartilage septum into two chambers (*nostrils or nares*). Air enters the nostrils through the right or left nostril *(naris)*. The nose, as well as the entire air pathway, is lined with *mucous membrane (mucosa),* which secretes mucus. *Turbinates* are bony projections within the nose. *Paranasal sinuses* surround the nose and secrete mucus that drains into the nasal passageway. (A diagram of the paranasal sinuses is shown in Figure 3.2.) *Adenoids* are a specialized mass of tissue located posteriorly in the nose.

◆ **MOUTH:** Air, as well as food, enters the mouth. The roof of the mouth has landmarks known as the *hard and soft palates.* Laterally and posteriorly in the mouth are the specialized structures known as the *tonsils.*

◆ **PHARYNX:** This organ is commonly called the throat. The pharynx is divided into three regions:

> *Nasopharynx*—the region behind the nose. The eustachian tube from the ear opens into the nasopharynx.

> *Oropharynx*—the region in back of the mouth.

> *Laryngopharynx*—the region of the voice box, just before the branching to separate the air pathway from the food pathway.

◆ **LARYNX:** This is the organ known as the voice box. It is here that a cartilage known as the *epiglottis* prevents food from entering the air pathways.

◆ **TRACHEA:** The trachea, commonly known as the windpipe, is located in the midline of the neck and branches as it enters the chest region. The trachea is in front of the food pathway. Other structures in the neck (*cervical region*) are the lymph nodes, which are located particularly laterally and under the chin (*submandibular*). These enlarge when there is localized infection.

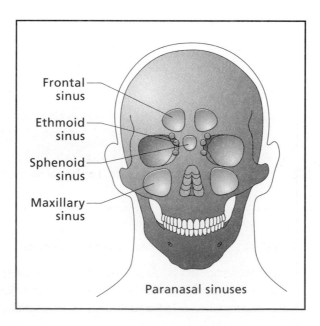

Figure 3.2 The Structures of the Paranasal Sinuses

- **BRONCHI:** The main air pathways branch (tree-like) off the trachea forming the right and left *bronchus (plural—bronchi)* within the lung.

- **BRONCHIOLES:** These are the smaller air pathways branching off the bronchi and ending in the alveoli.

- **ALVEOLI:** Within the lungs are the branching structures ending in the alveoli, or air sacs. The alveoli and their surrounding blood vessels are responsible for the exchange of gases (oxygen and carbon dioxide).

- **LUNGS:** The lungs are located in the chest (*thorax*). They are divided into sections called *lobes*. Each lung is contained within a lining called the *pleura*.

- **EARS:** The ear is placed in this system because of its close relationship to diseases of the respiratory system.

  The *external ear* collects sound waves that travel along the *external auditory canal,* which ends at the *tympanic membrane* (eardrum). Sound waves then enter the *middle ear*, where special structures pass along the sound waves. The *eustachian tube*, a pathway connecting to the nasopharynx, is located in the middle ear. The *labyrinth* (inner ear) contains the special nerve ends that pass these sound wave vibrations to the brain.

◆ CLINICAL ASSESSMENT

Assessment of the respiratory system includes the head, eyes, ears, nose, throat (HEENT), neck, and lungs.

- **EYES:** Eyes including the *conjunctivae* should be clear, not reddened, tearing, or mattery.

- **EARS:** The ears should be free of discharge; auditory canals should be clear without *cerumen;* and the tympanic membranes (TMs) should be flat, be pearly gray in color, have good light reflex, and have normal landmarks.

- **NOSE:** Nasal drainage should be clear if present.

- **MOUTH:** The oropharynx (mouth and throat) should be moist; tonsils (if present) should not be enlarged.

- **NECK:** There should be no cervical adenopathy.

- **LUNGS:** Lungs should be clear with good air entry. Breath sounds should be normal without rales, rhonchi, rubs, or wheezes.

The heart and abdomen are frequently included in the examination, even though the chief complaint refers to the respiratory system.

◆ METHODS OF EXAMINATION

The following methods of examination are used:

OBSERVATION: The examiner observes the color of the skin and nails; the contour and movement of the chest; and whether there are clubbing of the fingers, distended neck veins, or enlarged lymph nodes.

PERCUSSION: Percussing, or tapping, on the chest produces sounds indicating solid organs (*viscera*) as well as the presence of air.

PALPATION: The examiner is able to detect (feel) deficient movement of the chest.

AUSCULTATION: By listening to the chest, the examiner detects whether there is good air entry, the presence of fluid (*infiltrates*), and diminished air flow (*consolidation* or *obstruction*).

Different sounds and noises assist in determining which structures may be affected. For example, rhonchi may indicate bronchitis; rales may indicate bronchitis or small airway problems; crackling, or crepitus may point to involvement of lung tissue; and rubs may indicate pleural involvement.

Obtaining a history about a cough is very important, since it assists in determining where the problem occurs. The examiner asks whether the cough is dry, loose, productive or nonproductive of sputum, and what is the nature of the sputum. The appearance of sputum assists in making a diagnosis. For example, pink-tinged, rusty sputum may indicate bleeding and/or pneumonia; yellowish-green sputum is more common in bronchitis; and copious amounts of watery sputum are common in pulmonary congestion.

◆ SYMPTOMS AND DISEASE CONDITIONS

Practice word recognition and pronunciation; then spell each term.

adenopathy	(a´dĕ-nop´ă-thē)	enlargement of lymph nodes (also called *lymphadenopathy*)
asthma	(az´mă)	condition of lungs in which there is narrowing of air pathways resulting in difficulty breathing
barrel chested		having a rounded (barrel or box car) shape to chest
bronchitis	(brong-kī´tis)	inflammation in the bronchi
bronchospasm	(brong´kō-spazm)	contraction of bronchi, causing narrowing of the lumen (opening)
chronic obstructive pulmonary disease (COPD)		general term for diseases in which forced expiratory flow is slowed
congestion	(kon-jes´chŭn)	accumulation of abnormal amount of fluid or blood
cough	(kawf)	sudden forcing of air from respiratory tract
crackle	(krak´l)	sound in lungs similar to rolling hairs between fingers
croup	(krūp)	noisy, barklike respirations
dysphagia	(dis-fă´jē-ă)	difficulty swallowing
dyspnea	(disp-nē´ă)	difficulty breathing (dyspnea on exertion—refers to difficulty breathing during physical activity)
edema	(e-dē´mă)	accumulation of excess fluid in tissue
emphysema	(em-fi-sē´mă)	abnormal increase in size of air sacs (alveoli)

exacerbation	(eg-zas-er-bā´shŭn)	increase in symptom(s)
exudate	(eks´ū-dāt)	material deposited on tissue as a result of infection
fibrotic	(fī-brot´ik)	referring to tough or strong material
friction rub	(frik´shŭn)	grating or creaking sound when pleurae rub together
hoarse	(hōrs)	having a rough, harsh voice
hydration	(hī-drā´-shŭn)	adequate tissue fluid; not dehydrated
infiltrate	(in-fil´trāt)	material (fluid) deposited in tissue
injection	(in-jek´shŭn)	congestion or increase in fluid
low-grade fever		mildly elevated temperature
malaise	(mă-lāz´)	feeling of uneasiness; "out-of-sorts" feeling
orthopnea	(ōr-thop-nē´ă)	breathing discomfort when lying flat
otitis media	(ō-tī´tis mē´dē-ă)	inflammation of middle ear
pharyngitis	(far-in-jī´tis)	inflammation of pharynx (throat)
phlegm	(flem)	abnormal amounts of sticky mucus in the mouth and in the throat
pneumonia	(nū-mō´nē-ă)	inflammation of lung tissue
rales	(rahlz)	rattle heard on auscultation of chest
rhinitis	(rī-nī´tis)	inflammation of the nasal mucosa
rhinorrhea	(rī-nō-rē´ă)	runny nose
rhonchi	(rong´kī)	musical pitch heard on auscultation of chest
shotty nodes	(shot´ē)	BB-like (very tiny bumps) feeling of lymph nodes
sinusitis	(sī-nŭ-sī´tis)	inflammation of the sinuses
sputum	(spū´tŭm)	material raised from the lungs
suppurative	(sŭp´yŭr-ă-tiv)	forming pus (purulent material)
tachypnea	(tak-ip-nē´a)	increased rate of breathing
tonsillitis	(ton´si-lī´tis)	inflammation of the tonsils
upper respiratory tract infection (URI)		infection of upper air passages, not the lungs
wheeze	(hwēz)	whistling or squeaking sound when breathing

◆ LABORATORY TESTS

blood work	(hē-mō-glō´bin) (dif-er-en´shăl) (lim´fō-sītz) (mon´ō-sītz) (ē-ō-sin´ō-filz) (bā´sō-filz)	WBC (white blood cells); hemoglobin; differential (PMNs, lymphocytes, monocytes, eosinophils, basophils)
culture	(bā´tă strep-tō-kok´ŭs)	to "grow" a material in order to identify the micro-organism; for example, group A Beta streptococcus (frequently called Quick Strep or Rapid Strep test)
mono test	(mon´ō) (mon´ō-nū-klē-ō´sis)	blood test for infectious mononucleosis

◆ X-RAY PROCEDURES

Chest X rays: Chest films are generally taken in the PA (*posteroanterior*) view; a lateral view may also be ordered.

Sinus films: Sinus films are used to detect normal translucency or opacity (*clouding*).

◆ MEDICAL PROCEDURES

inhaler	(in-hāl´er)	device used by patient to inhale medications
nebulization	(neb´yū-li-zā´shŭn)	treatment using a spray
spirometry	(spī-rom´ĕ-trē)	pulmonary function test (PFT) that determines how well the lungs are functioning and helps determine causes of shortness of breath. It includes FVC (forced vital capacity) and FEV1 (forced expiratory volume in one second).
tympanometry	(tim-pan´om-ĕ´trē) (tim-pan-ō´gram)	test to check how well the eardrums function; record is called a tympanogram
vaporizer	(vā´per-īz-er)	device to add moisture to the air (steamer or humidifier)

◆ SURGICAL PROCEDURES

myringotomy	(mir-ing-got´ŏ-mē)	incision into eardrum
PE tubes		tiny polyethylene tubes placed in ear for drainage
tonsillectomy and adenoidectomy (TA)	(ton´si-lek´tō-mē) (ad´ĕ-noy-dek´tō-mē)	excision of tonsils and adenoids

◆ MEDICATIONS

albuterol (Trade names Proventil and Ventolin)	(al-byū´ter-ol)	bronchodilator
Augmentin	(aug-ment´in)	antibiotic
Azmacort	(as´mah-kort)	corticosteroid for asthma
Bactrim	(bak´trim)	antibiotic
Bicillin	(bī´sil-in)	antibiotic
Pediazole	(pē´dē-ă-zol)	antibiotic
Prednisone	(pred´ni-sōn)	cortisone
Robitussin	(rō-bi-tus´in)	antitussive
Tylenol	(tī´len-ol)	analgesic

◆ MISCELLANEOUS TERMS

audible	(ah´da-bul)	able to be heard
bulging	(bul´jing)	swelling
consolidation	(kon-sol´ĕ-dā´shŭn)	condition of becoming solid

cryptic	(krip´tik)	hidden
diffuse	(di-fyūs´)	spread out
discrete	(dis-krēt´)	separate; distinct
extruding	(eks-trūd´ing)	in a position of being pushed out
gaunt	(gont)	thin and bony; emaciated
nocturnal	(nok-ter´năl)	occurring at night
patent	(pa´tent)	open
retraction	(rē-trak´shŭn)	drawing inward
supple	(sŭp´l)	easily moveable

TRANSCRIPTION CHECKOFF SHEET
by Patient

Worksheet 100

transcription 94

DOCTOR DICTATING:	Debra Litman, M.D.
TYPE OF DICTATION:	Chart notes, letters, and X-ray reports
DATE OF TRANSCRIPTION:	April 10, 19--

Item Number	Patient	Date Started	Date Completed	Grade/ Number of Errors
1	Ronald Myers			
2	Andrea Sandstrom			
3	Jordan Adams			
4	Anthony Walters			
5	Jack Manly			
6	Megan Trost			
7	Norman Jenson			
8	Claudia Stein			
9	Tina Langley			
10	Leonard Reichart			
11	Michael Hite			
12	Duane Lofgren			
13	Sandra Longworth			
14	Charles Jefferson			
15	Ruth Hardy			
16	Ryan Chadsworth			

4 ◆ THE CARDIOVASCULAR SYSTEM

◆ **CARDIOVASCULAR SYSTEM FUNCTION AND COMPONENTS**

The cardiovascular system includes the heart, blood, blood and lymphatic vessels, lymph tissue, and the spleen. This system is the transportation system of the body.

Functions of this system include the following:

◆ **NUTRITION:** This is achieved by the transportation of glucose, protein, minerals, and fats to the body cells.

◆ **EXCRETION:** Excretion is the process by which metabolic wastes are eliminated from the body's cells.

◆ **PROTECTION:** Protection is provided by the transportation of antibodies for resistance.

◆ **REGULATION OF BODY FLUIDS:** This function helps balance the body's temperature.

◆ **RESPIRATION:** Respiration provides for the transportation of oxygen and carbon dioxide.

Blood has the following components:

The *erythrocytes* (red blood cells) contain the *hemoglobin* which carries oxygen. The normal hemoglobin value is listed as 14 to 16 grams per 100 cubic centimeters (cc) of blood.

Leukocytes (white blood cells) assist in fighting infections, respond to allergens, and destroy foreign cells; the normal count is 5,000 to 10,000. There are several kinds of white cells including the polymorphonuclears (*PMNs*), *lymphocytes, monocytes, eosinophils,* and *basophils*. Counting these cells individually is referred to as a *differential* count.

Another component is *platelets* (*thrombocytes*) whose function is blood clotting. The *plasma* (liquid part) transports water, nutrients, hormones, salts, and several kinds of proteins.

The function of the heart is to pump the blood so it will circulate throughout the body. The heart is located in the *mediastinum* (middle of the chest). It is a double pump. The right side receives carbon dioxide from the body cells and sends it to the lungs, where it is exchanged for oxygen. Then this oxygen-rich blood returns to the left side of the heart. The left side pumps the blood out to the body cells to deliver the oxygen. Actually, both sides pump at the same time, but the blood goes in different directions and is prevented from flowing backward by *valves*. The heart beats (pumps) 60 to 80 times per minute. Because the heart is a muscle, it requires its own blood supply, which is obtained through *coronary circulation*.

The blood is transported through a series of vessels. *Arteries* carry blood away from the heart, *veins* carry blood to the heart, and *capillaries* surround body cells and do the exchange mechanism with oxygen, carbon dioxide, nutrients, and wastes. There are several arterial locations throughout the body

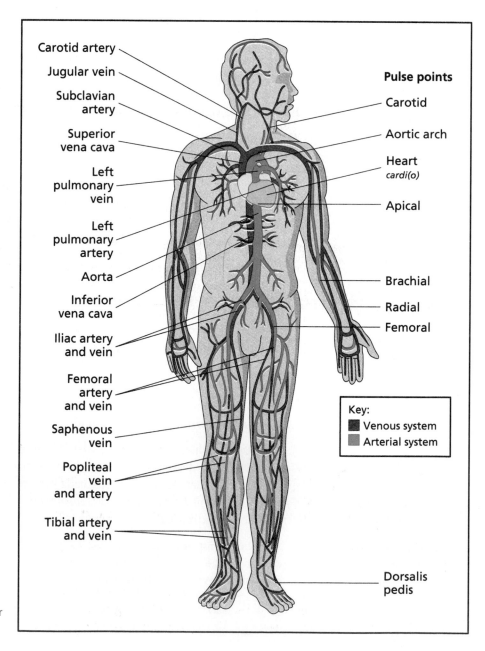

Pulse points

Carotid artery
Jugular vein
Subclavian artery
Superior vena cava
Left pulmonary vein
Left pulmonary artery
Aorta
Inferior vena cava
Iliac artery and vein
Femoral artery and vein
Saphenous vein
Popliteal vein and artery
Tibial artery and vein

Carotid
Aortic arch
Heart
cardi(o)
Apical
Brachial
Radial
Femoral
Dorsalis pedis

Key:
Venous system
Arterial system

Figure 4.1 The Cardiovascular System

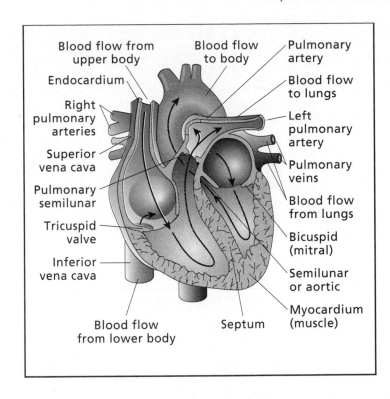

Right pulmonary arteries

Blood flow from upper body

Endocardium

Blood flow to body

Pulmonary artery

Blood flow to lungs

Left pulmonary artery

Superior vena cava

Pulmonary veins

Pulmonary semilunar

Blood flow from lungs

Tricuspid valve

Bicuspid (mitral)

Inferior vena cava

Semilunar or aortic

Blood flow from lower body

Septum

Myocardium (muscle)

Figure 4.2 Flow of Blood through the Heart

where the heartbeat (*pulse*) can be felt. *Blood pressure* is a measure of the amount of force (*systole*) of the heart pumping the blood through an artery and the relaxation, or filling phase (*diastole,*) of the heart chambers.

The lymphatic system is a series of vessels and lymph tissue located throughout the body to assist in the transportation mechanism as well as the filtering of foreign particles from the blood. The lymph tissue is referred to as *nodes*, or glands. Tonsils and adenoids are lymph tissue.

The spleen, located in the upper left quadrant of the abdomen and protected by the ribs, manufactures some white blood cells and antibodies as well as salvaging usable iron from the blood stream.

Figure 4.1 shows the larger arteries and veins and the pulse points. Refer to additional references (Appendix A) for more definitive diagrams.

Circulation Through the Heart

Follow the circulation of blood through the heart shown in Figure 4.2. Blood returns from body cells via the superior and inferior vena cavae, empties into the right atrium, passes through a valve into the right ventricle, and is pumped to lungs via the pulmonary arteries. Oxygenated blood returns via the pulmonary veins into the left atrium, passes through the mitral valve into the left ventricle, and is pumped out the aorta to the body's cells.

◆ CLINICAL ASSESSMENT

The examiner checks heart rate and rhythm. A normal rhythm is referred to as "normal sinus rhythm" (referring to the SA node of the heart). There are several heart sounds made as the blood flows through the valves and as they snap shut. The first and second sounds (S1 and S2, respectively) refer to the closing of the mitral and tricuspid valves, and then the aortic and pulmonary valves. A third sound (S3) may be heard in children. An S4 is an abnormal sound, as are murmurs, gallops, and rubs. Murmurs may be systolic or diastolic and are described according to loudness on a grading system with a scale of I to VI, with VI being the loudest.

Blood pressure may be considered high when the systolic pressure is consistently more than 150 or the diastolic more than 100. Normally, there is little difference in the reading if the patient changes position. Fluctuations could indicate a symptom requiring evaluation.

Peripheral pulses should be palpable, equal, and symmetric. They are frequently graded as 2+ (*two plus*, which is a normal grade). There should be no leg, ankle, or pedal (foot) edema.

◆ SYMPTOMS AND DISEASE CONDITIONS

Practice word recognition and pronunciation; then spell each term:

anemia	(ă-nē´mē-ă)	low hemoglobin
angina	(an´ji-nā)	constricting chest pain
arteriosclerotic heart disease (ASHD)	(ar-tēr´ē-ō-skler-ot´ik)	hardening of the coronary arteries
bradycardia	(brad-ē-kar´dē-ă)	slow pulse
bruit	(brū-ē´)	murmur
congestive heart failure (CHF)	(kon-jes´tiv)	increased fluid especially in lungs due to poor circulation
coronary artery disease	(kōr´o-nār-ē)	disease affecting blood vessels that supply heart muscle
deep venous thrombosis (DVT)	(vē´nŭs throm-bō´sis)	formation of blood clots in veins
dysrhythmia	(dis-rith´mē-ă)	abnormal heart rhythm; arrhythmia
epistaxis	(ep´i-stak´sis)	nosebleed
fatigue	(fă-tēg´)	feeling of tiredness
hemorrhage	(hem´ō-rij)	bleeding not easily stopped; excessive bleeding
hemorrhoids	(hem´ō-roydz)	dilated veins in rectal area
hypercholesterolemia	(hī´per-kō-les´ter-ol-ē´mē-ă)	increased amount of cholesterol (fatty substances) in the blood
hypertension	(hī´per-ten´shŭn)	high blood pressure
murmur	(mer´mer)	abnormal heart sound coming from heart valves
myocardial infarction (MI)	(mī-ō-kar´dē-ăl in-fark´shŭn)	inadequate blood supply to heart muscle; heart attack
occlusion	(ŏ´klū´zhŭn)	the state of being closed
palpitation	(pal-pi-tā´shŭn)	patient's awareness of heartbeat
stenosis	(ste-nō´sis)	narrowing of blood vessel
tachycardia	(tak´i-kar´dē-ă)	rapid heartbeat
thrombophlebitis	(throm´bō-flĕ-bī´tis)	inflammation of vein due to blood clot
thrombosis	(throm-bō´sis)	blood clot
varicose veins	(vār´i-kōs)	enlarged, tortuous veins
vascular insufficiency	(vas´kyū-lăr)	inadequate blood vessels

◆ LABORATORY TESTS

Laboratory studies are performed for the diagnosis of many conditions. Tests that are used in the transcription of this chapter are listed here (refer to Appendix E for detailed explanations):

chemistries including		
electrolytes	(ē-lek´trō-lītz)	sodium, potassium
chlorides	(klōr´īds)	
creatinine	(krē-at´i-nēn)	
complete blood count (CBC)		
hemoglobin	(hē-mō-glō´bin)	
red blood cell count (RBC)		
white blood cell count (WBC)		
and differential	(dif-er-en´shăl)	
lipid profile to include	(lip´ed)	
cholesterol	(kō-les´ter-ol)	
prothrombin time	(prō-throm´bin)	
blood coagulation time	(kō-ag-yū-lā´shŭn)	

◆ MEDICAL PROCEDURES

Doppler ultrasound	(dop´ler)	use of sound waves to detect blood clot
electrocardiogram (ECG or EKG)	(ē-lek-trō-kar´dē-ō-gram)	graphic recording of heart's electrical activity to give information about rhythm, size, and damage to heart muscle. The cycle includes waves referred to as *P, Q, R, S,* and *T*.
Holter monitor	(hōl´ter)	continuous recording during normal activities; ambulatory EKG
stress (exercise) EKG		graphic recording that evaluates heart's response during physical activity (such as a treadmill)
ventriculogram	(ven-trik´yū-lō-gram)	recording of ventricular activity

◆ SURGICAL PROCEDURES

angioplasty	(an´jē-ō-plas-tē)	reconstruction of a vessel
cardiac catheterization	(kath´ĕ-ter-ī-zā´shŭn)	insertion of tube into heart
coronary artery bypass graft (CABG)		replacement (graft) of damaged coronary artery

◆ MEDICATIONS

Advil (ibuprofen)	(ī-bū´prō-fen)	NSAID, analgesic
Americaine	(ă-mer´ĭ-kān)	analgesic
amiodarone	(am-ē-ō´dar-ōn)	antiarrhythmic
aspirin	(as´pi-rin)	analgesic
atenolol	(ă-ten´ō-lōl)	antihypertensive, antianginal

Ativan	(ăt´ĭ-van)	anxiolytic
Cardizem	(kar´dĭ-zem)	antianginal
Coumadin	(kū´mă-din)	anticoagulant
Demerol	(dem´er-ol)	narcotic analgesic
enalapril	(n-ăl´ă-pryl)	antihypertensive
Lanoxin	(lan-ok´sin)	antiarrhythmic
(digoxin)	(di-jok´sin)	
Lasix	(lā´siks)	diuretic
lidocaine	(lī´dō-kān)	anesthetic
(Xylocaine)	(zī´lō-kān)	
Marcaine	(mar´kān)	anesthetic
nitroglycerin	(nī-trō-glis´er-in)	antianginal
Percocet	(per´kō-set)	narcotic analgesic
Procardia	(prō-kar´dē-ă)	antianginal
Vistaril	(viz´tar-yl)	anxiolytic

◆ MISCELLANEOUS TERMS

aggravating	(ag´ră-vāt-ing)	making worse
alleviating	(ă-lē´vē-ā´ting)	lessening; relieving
deviates	(dē´vē-āts)	turns aside
extremity	(eks-trem´i-tē)	arm or leg
fingerbreadth	(fin´ger-bredth)	width of a finger; almost an inch
fleeting	(flēt´ing)	passing swiftly
hyperkinesis	(hī´per-ki-nē´sis)	increased muscular movement
inverted	(in-ver´ted)	changed to opposite direction
lightheadedness	(līt-hed´ed-ness)	dizziness
modalities	(mō-dal´i-tēz)	forms, methods
obliteration	(ob-lit-er-ā´shŭn)	blotting out; destruction
ostium	(os´tē-ŭm)	opening
reflexes	(rē´flek-ez)	involuntary movements
sublingual	(sŭb-ling´gwăl)	under the tongue
TED (thromboembolic disease) stockings		elastic support hose
tingly	(ting´lē)	prickly sensation
tremulous	(trem´yū-lŭs)	quivering

WS - 94
T - 93 94

TRANSCRIPTION CHECKOFF SHEET
by Patient

DOCTOR DICTATING: Lynn Solinski, M.D., and Lee W. Kim, M.D.

TYPE OF DICTATION: Chart notes, history and physicals, and letter

DATE OF TRANSCRIPTION: April 12, 19--

Item Number	Patient	Date Started	Date Completed	Grade/ Number of Errors
1	Alyssa Babcock			
2	Betty Forsman			
3	Marietta Henley			
4	Renee Eckstrom			
5	Donald Eickten			
6	Bryant Andres			
7	Derek Wood			
8	Trent Wilson			
9	Ali Saarken			

THE DIGESTIVE SYSTEM

◆ DIGESTIVE SYSTEM FUNCTION AND COMPONENTS

The digestive system has the following functions:

- ◆ **INGESTION:** The process of taking nutrients and/or substances and water into the system is known as ingestion.

- ◆ **DIGESTION:** This is the breaking down of ingested material into substances that the body can use.

- ◆ **ABSORPTION:** Absorption is the process of taking in nutrients and other substances into the blood stream.

- ◆ **METABOLISM:** The subsequent breakdown and rebuilding of substances so they will be accepted by the body cells is known as metabolism.

- ◆ **ELIMINATION:** Elimination is the getting rid of the waste products that cannot be used by the body cells.

Food nutrients have the following classifications and uses:

- *Carbohydrates* are used for energy.

- *Proteins* build tissues.

- *Fats* are broken down and stored for energy and insulation.

- *Minerals* are needed for metabolism, bone formation, and nerve functioning.

- *Vitamins* are important for metabolism and general overall health maintenance.

Water is essential in the diet to help transport these nutrients in the blood stream.

The digestive (gastrointestinal, or GI) tract is a continuous pathway from the mouth to the anus and includes the following organs:

- **Mouth:** This organ is used for ingestion and for the mechanical and chemical breakdown of food.

- **Esophagus:** This serves as a pathway for food coming from the mouth.

- **Stomach:** This cavity is where digestion and the chemical breakdown of foodstuffs takes place.

- **Intestine (bowel):** This tubular pathway is where digestive juices, or enzymes, continue the breakdown of food particles and where absorption takes place.

The first part (small intestine) consists of the *duodenum*, the *jejunum*, and the *ileum*.

The last section of the bowel is the large intestine, or colon, which is divided into sections according to landmarks:

The *cecum*, a C-shaped region in the lower right abdomen.

The *ascending colon*, going up the right side of the abdomen.

The *transverse colon*, going across the upper abdomen.

The *descending colon*, going down the left side of abdomen.

The *sigmoid*, the S-shaped region in the left lower side.

The *rectum*, which is the last 6 to 8 inches of the colon.

In addition to these main organs, there are accessory organs that help with the digestive process. These include the *salivary glands* in the mouth, which add saliva that contains water (for moisture) and digestive enzymes. The *liver* manufactures bile, which is necessary for the metabolism of fats. The *gallbladder* stores the bile. The *pancreas* produces insulin for carbohydrate metabolism and digestive enzymes. The appendix is a structure off the cecum; it has no function.

◆ ANATOMICAL LANDMARKS

The following terms apply to the digestive anatomical structure:

◆ **ABDOMEN** is the region between the diaphragm and the pelvis (between the hip bones). The abdomen can be divided into quadrants as a method of locating symptoms: left and right upper quadrants (LUQ and RUQ, respectively) and left and right lower quadrants (LLQ and RLQ, respectively).

◆ **EPIGASTRIUM** is the upper middle region of the abdomen over the stomach (*gastrium*).

◆ **UPPER GI TRACT** refers to the stomach and duodenum.

◆ **LOWER GI TRACT** is also known as the colon and includes the area from the cecum to the rectum.

◆ **PERITONEUM** is the apronlike membrane lining the abdominal cavity.

Follow the digestive pathway in Figure 5.1, noting which organs the substances pass through from the mouth to the anus.

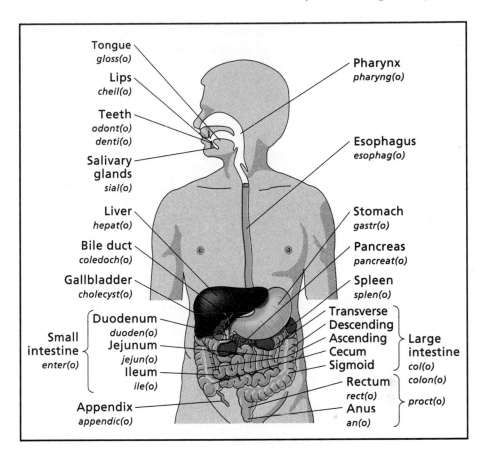

Figure 5.1 The Digestive System

◆ CLINICAL ASSESSMENT

An examination of the mouth includes teeth, tongue, mucous membranes, and breath.

The patient's history relating to the esophagus and stomach includes symptoms of appetite, nausea, vomiting, pain (where, when, how long, and its character), food intolerance, flatulence, and heartburn.

Symptoms that relate to the intestine include pain, constipation, diarrhea, and bleeding.

A visual examination includes palpation to note tenderness, rigidity, organ enlargement, or masses. Auscultation is used mainly to detect whether or not bowel sounds are present.

Stool (*feces, BM*) is normally brown in color because of the by-products of the digestive process. The anatomy of the intestine gives stool its characteristic shape and size.

◆ SYMPTOMS AND DISEASE CONDITIONS

Practice word recognition and pronunciation; then spell each term.

alcoholism	(al´kō-hol-izm)	chronic, excessive drinking of alcohol
anorexia	(an-ō-rek´sē-ǎ)	diminished appetite
appendicitis	(ǎ-pen-di-sī´tis)	inflammation of appendix
belch	(belsh)	burp
buccal	(bŭk´ǎl)	inside surface of cheek

cholecystitis	(kō´lē-sis-tī´tis)	inflammation of gallbladder
cholelithiasis	(kō´lē-li-thī´ă-sis)	stones in gallbladder
cirrhosis	(sir-rō´sis)	progressive liver disease
clay-colored stool		no color to stool
colic	(kol´ik)	spasmodic abdominal pain (adjective—colicky)
constipation	(kon-sti-pā´shŭn)	infrequent hard, dry stool
Crohn's disease	(krōnz)	inflammation and/or ulcer formation in ileum
diarrhea	(dī-ă-rē´ă)	frequent watery or nonformed stool
diverticulum	(dī-ver-tik´yū-lŭm)	pouch in intestine
dyspepsia	(dis-pep´sē-ă)	indigestion
dysphagia	(dis-fă´jē-ă)	difficulty swallowing
emesis	(em´ĕ-sis)	vomiting
flatulence or flatus	(flat´yū-lens, flā´tŭs)	excessive gas in GI tract
gastritis	(gas-trī´tis)	inflammation of stomach
gastroenteritis	(gas´trō-en-ter-ī´tis)	inflammation of stomach and intestine
hematemesis	(hē-mă-tem´ĕ-sis)	vomiting blood
hematochezia	(hē´mă-tō-kē´zē-ă)	bloody stools
hepatitis	(hep-ă-tī´tis)	inflammation of liver
hernia	(her´nē-ă)	protrusion of an organ
hiatal hernia	(hī-ā´tăl)	protrusion of part of stomach through diaphragm
hypokalemia	(hī´pō-ka-lē´mē-ă)	decreased potassium in blood
icterus	(ik´ter-ŭs)	jaundice; yellowish color to skin or eyes
ileus	(il´ē-ŭs)	bowel obstruction
malaise	(mă-lāz´)	out-of-sorts feeling; general discomfort
melena	(me-lē´nă)	dark, tarry stools
nausea	(naw´zē-ă)	feeling of having to vomit
palpitations	(pal-pi-tā´shŭnz)	patient's awareness of heart beating
pancreatitis	(pan´krē-ă-tī´tis)	inflammation of pancreas
polyp	(pol´ip)	projecting tissue mass
reflux	(rē´flŭks)	backward flow
stricture	(strik´chūr)	narrowing
thrush	(thrŭsh)	fungal or yeast infection of mouth tissue, frequently occurring after treatment with antibiotics
ulcer	(ŭl´ser)	open sore

◆ LABORATORY TESTS

Blood tests for the digestive system include the following:

alkaline phosphatase	(al´kă-lĭn fos´fă-tās)
amylase	(am´il-ās)
bilirubin	(bil-i-rū´bin)
BUN (blood urea nitrogen)	(yū-rē´ă)
calcium	
CBC	
creatinine	(krē-at´i-nēn)
electrolytes (sodium, potassium, chloride, and CO2)	

glucose   (glū´kōs)
SGOT/AST
A stool test for the digestive system is the hemoccult or guaiac (gwī´ak) test,
which checks for blood in the stool specimen.

◆ X-RAY TESTS

X rays include the following for the digestive system:

barium enema	(ba´rē-ŭm en´ĕ-mă)	documents presence of colon disease
flat plate of abdomen		evaluates suspected blockage or perforation of intestine (no contrast material or dye is used)
upper gastrointestinal (upper GI series or UGI)		outlines upper digestive tract for diseases such as ulcers. This test may include a barium swallow to examine the esophagus and/or may include a small bowel follow-through to examine the jejunum and ileum.

◆ MEDICAL PROCEDURES

colonoscopy	(kō-lon-os´kō-pē)	visualization of the colon with a scope instrument
endoscopy	(en-dos´kŏ-pē)	general term for visualization using scope
flexible sigmoidoscopy	(sig´moy-dos´kō-pē)	visualization of the sigmoid using flexible scope
ultrasound	(ŭl´tră-sownd)	imaging using sound waves to detect liquid or solid mass and tissue

◆ SURGICAL PROCEDURES

appendectomy	(ap-pen-dek´tō-mē)	removal of appendix
cholecystectomy	(kō´lē-sis-tek´tō-mē)	removal of gallbladder
gastric resection	(gas´trik rē-sek´shŭn)	removal of part of stomach
gastric bypass		rerouting pathway to bypass some of stomach region, commonly done by stapling part of stomach
laparoscopy	(lap-ă-ros´kō-pē)	visualization with fiberoptic instrument through the abdominal wall via tiny incision
laparotomy	(lap-ă-rot´ō-mē)	incision through abdominal wall

◆ MEDICATIONS

Carafate	(kar´ă-fāt)	antiulcer
chlorpheniramine	(klōr´fĕn-ir´ă-mēn)	decongestant
Enfamil	(n´fă-mil)	baby formula
K-Dur	(k´dur)	potassium supplement
Lanoxin	(lan-ok´sin)	antiarrhythmic

Lomotil	(lō-mō´til)	antidiarrheal
Maalox	(mā´lox)	antacid
Metamucil	(met´ă-mū-sil)	laxative
Milk of Magnesia	(mag-nē´zhŭh)	laxative
Motrin	(mō-trin)	analgesic
Mycelex troches	(mī´sel-x trō´kes)	antifungal
Mylanta	(mī-lan´ta)	antacid
Prednisone	(pred´ni-sōn)	cortisone
Prilosec	(pril´ō-sik)	antiulcer
Tagamet	(tāg´ă-met)	antiulcer
Tenormin	(ten-or´min)	antihypertensive, antianginal
Toradol	(tor´ă-dol)	analgesic
Zantac	(zan´tak)	antiulcer

◆ MISCELLANEOUS TERMS

antispasmodic	(an´tē-spaz-mod´ik)	able to decrease or stop spasms or cramps
claustrophobia	(klaw-strō-fō´bē-ă)	morbid fear of confinement
costovertebral angle	(kos-tō-ver´tĕ-brăl)	area where ribs meet vertebrae and the kidneys are located
digital	(dij´i-tăl)	relating to fingers or toes
GI cocktail		blend of antacid and anesthetic
nonsteroidal	(non-stēr´oy-dăl)	containing no cortisone medication
occult	(ŏ-kŭlt´)	hidden
retroflexed	(re´trō-flekst)	bent backward
screening		testing
sessile	(ses´il)	having a broad base

TRANSCRIPTION CHECKOFF SHEET
by Patient

WS 100
T-93

DOCTOR DICTATING: Lynn Solinski, M.D., and Debra Litman, M.D.

TYPE OF DICTATION: Chart notes, letter, procedure notes, and X-ray report

DATE OF TRANSCRIPTION: April 15, 19--

Item Number	Patient	Date Started	Date Completed	Grade/ Number of Errors
1	Carol Gregg			
2	Julie Kurland			
3	Jeanne Raymond			
4	Cecil Razido			
5	Laura Eagan			
6	Brian Bruder			
7	Harriet Myers			
8	Philip Purnell			
9	Lynn Kelly			
10	Edwina Forrester			
11	Bruce Noreen			

6 ◆ THE ENDOCRINE SYSTEM

◆ ENDOCRINE SYSTEM FUNCTION AND COMPONENTS

The function of the endocrine system is to produce *hormones*. Hormones are chemicals that regulate the body's activities. They are sent directly into the blood stream and circulated throughout the body. These hormones are interrelated, and their effects overlap. The endocrine system and the nervous system work together to regulate body processes—the first producing long-term effects; the other producing short-term action.

The main components of the endocrine system, as shown in Figure 6.1, include the following:

◆ **PITUITARY GLAND:** The *pituitary gland,* located in the head, is the master gland. It regulates many of the other organs, such as the thyroid gland, the reproductive glands, the adrenal glands, the kidneys, and the uterus, as well as the general functioning of the body.

◆ **THYROID GLAND:** The *thyroid gland* is located in the neck around the trachea. Its main function is regulating the body's metabolism.

◆ **PARATHYROID GLANDS:** Located on the thyroid, the hormones from these glands affect the body's use of calcium.

◆ **ADRENAL GLANDS:** The *adrenal glands* are located on top of the kidneys. The hormones from these glands respond in times of physiologic stress (disease) and affect kidney function and sexual development.

◆ **ISLETS OF LANGERHANS:** Within the pancreas, the islets produce insulin, which is necessary for the body's cells to accept glucose.

◆ **OVARIES AND TESTES:** The *ovaries* and *testes* are also part of this system, but their functions are discussed in Chapter 8, which covers the reproductive system.

A brief summary of some common hormones is shown here:

Gland	Hormone	Effect
pituitary	thyrotrophin (TSH)	thyroid gland
	adrenocorticotrophin	adrenals
thyroid	thyroxine (T3 and T4)	body's metabolism
parathyroids	parahormone	use of calcium

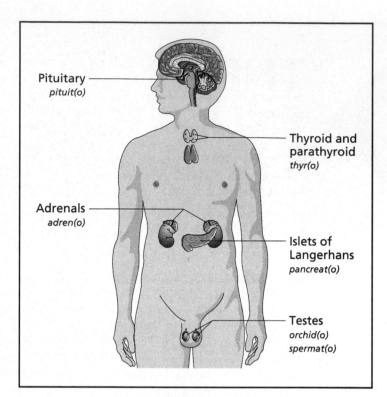

Figure 6.1 Male Endocrine System

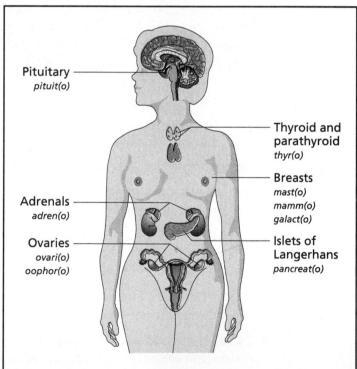

Figure 6.2 Female Endocrine System

Gland	Hormone	Effect
adrenals	cortisone	physiologic stress
	epinephrine	physiologic stress
islets of Langerhans	insulin	use of glucose
testes	testosterone	male sex features
ovaries	estrogen	female sex features
	progesterone	menstrual cycle

◆ CLINICAL ASSESSMENT

Two organs that commonly malfunction in this system are the pancreas and the thyroid. The examiner asks questions regarding symptoms of excessive sweating, weight gain or loss, increased thirst, changes in vision, and increased urination.

Two of the most common disease conditions of this system are thyroid diseases and diabetes. Thyroid conditions affect the thinking processes, energy levels, the body's temperature, the digestive and reproductive processes, and the eyes. Diabetes also affects the entire system including the kidneys, the nerves (including vision), and the cardiovascular system and circulation, especially of the lower extremities. Thus, the physical exam may include assessment of many of these organs and functions.

◆ SYMPTOMS AND DISEASE CONDITIONS

Practice word recognition and pronunciation; then spell each term.

diabetes mellitus	(dī-ă-bē´tēz mel´ĭ-tus)	poorly functioning pancreas resulting in inadequate insulin production or inability of body cells to utilize carbohydrates Type I: originates in childhood; Type II: comes on in adulthood
diaphoresis	(dī´ă-fō-rē´sis)	excessive sweating; profuse perspiration
discrete	(dis-krēt´)	separate; distinct
euthyroid	(yū-thī´royd)	normally functioning thyroid gland
exophthalmos or exophthalmus	(ek-sof-thal´mos)	bulging eyes
glycosuria	(glī´kō-sū´rē-ă)	glucose (sugar) in urine
goiter	(goy´ter)	enlargement of thyroid gland
Graves' disease	(grāvz)	overactive thyroid characterized by goiter
hypercholesterolemia	(hī´per-kō-les´ter-ol-ē´mē-ă)	increased cholesterol in blood
hyperglycemia	(hī´per-glī-sē´mē-ă)	too much glucose in the blood; high blood sugar
hypertension	(hī-per-ten´shŭn)	high blood pressure
hyperthyroidism	(hī-per-thī´royd-izm)	excessive functioning activity of thyroid
hypoglycemia	(hī´pō-glī-sē´mē-ă)	too little glucose in blood; low blood sugar
hypothyroidism	(hī-pō-thī´royd-izm)	deficiency of thyroid function
nephropathy	(ne-frop´ă-thē)	kidney disease
neuropathy	(nū-rop´-ă-thē)	disease involving nerves
polydipsia	(pol-ē-dip´sē-ă)	increased thirst
polyphagia	(pol-ē-fā´jē-ă)	increased appetite
polyuria	(pol-ē-yū´rē-ă)	excessive urination
proteinuria	(prō-tē-nū´rē-ă)	protein in urine
stasis ulcer	(stā´sis)	ulcer due to poor blood flow
thyrotoxicosis	(thī´rō-tok-si-kō´sis)	extreme overactivity of thyroid gland

◆ LABORATORY TESTS

Diabetes: Accu-Chek/Chemstrip
                            glucose (blood sugar)—random, fasting, post prandial (pran´dē-ăl)

	glucose tolerance	
	hemoglobin A1c	
Thyroid disease:	T3, T4, TSH	
Kidney function:	24-hour urine for creatinine clearance	
	creatinine	
	total protein	
Other lab tests:		
	potassium	
	cholesterols	(HDL, LDL) (kō-les′ter-ōls)
	lipids	(lip′eds)
	triglycerides	(trī-glis′erīds)

◆ MEDICAL PROCEDURES

ablation therapy	(ab-lā′shŭn)	
or ablative therapy	(ab-lā′tiv)	destruction of tissue

◆ SURGICAL PROCEDURES

thyroidectomy	(thī-roy-dek′tō-mē)	excision of the thyroid

◆ MEDICATIONS

atenolol	(ă-ten′ō-lol)	antihypertensive, antianginal
Duoderm	(dū′ō-derm)	wound dressing, occlusive
Estraderm	(s′tra-derm)	hormone estrogen
glyburide	(glī′byū-rīd)	antidiabetic
Imipramine	(im-ip′ră-mēn)	antidepressant
Insulin:		
Humulin	(hyū′mū-lin)	hormone
NPH		
regular		
levothyroxine	(lē′vō-thī-rok′sēn)	hormone
lisinopril	(līs-in′ō-pril)	antihypertensive
Neosporin	(nē-ō-spor′in)	antibiotic
Premarin	(prem′ar-in)	hormone estrogen
PTU (propylthiouracil)	(prō′pil-thī-ō-yū′ră-sil)	thyroid inhibitor
radioactive iodine		thyroid inhibitor
Synthroid	(sin′throyd)	hormone
Zoloft	(zō′loft)	antidepressant

◆ MISCELLANEOUS TERMS

fluctuate	(flŭk′tyū-āt)	to vary
funduscopic	(fŭn′dŭs-skōp′-ik)	characterized by visualization of interior of eye

intervention	(in-ter-ven´shŭn)	treatment to alter or change course
normotensive	(nōr-mō-ten´siv)	normal blood pressure
scarred	(skard)	replacement of normal tissue by fibrous tissue after an injury
suboptimal	(sŭb-op´ti-măl)	less than desired

6

WS-100
T-89

TRANSCRIPTION CHECKOFF SHEET
by Patient

DOCTOR DICTATING: Lynn Solinski, M.D.

TYPE OF DICTATION: Chart notes and letter

DATE OF TRANSCRIPTION: April 15, 19--

Item Number	Patient	Date Started	Date Completed	Grade/ Number of Errors
1	Russell Hendricks			
2	Randy LaMotta			
3	Luis Diaz			
4	Seymour Teke			
5	Ludwig Grandquist			
6	Robert Bias			
7	Tashia Bealka			
8	Barbara Glickstein			
9	Irene Colbert			
10	Tia Wytkoff			
11	Darla Garske			

7 ◆ THE URINARY SYSTEM

◆ URINARY SYSTEM FUNCTION AND COMPONENTS

The function of the urinary system is to produce urine and eliminate it from the body. This may be thought of as the process of cleaning or clearing the blood of waste products. Symptoms of malfunction can range from negligible to life-threatening if the kidneys "shut down."

Functions of this system, in this production of urine, include the following:

- Regulation of volume and electrolyte concentration of the body's fluids.

- Elimination of waste products.

- Regulation of blood pressure.

As shown in Figure 7.1, the urinary systems has the following organs:

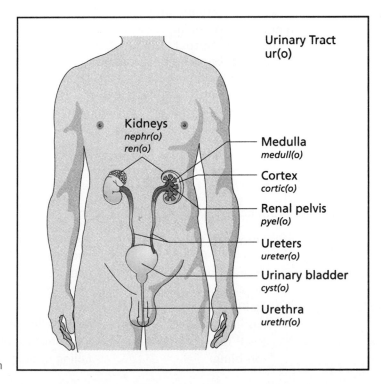

Figure 7.1 The Urinary System

◆ **KIDNEYS:** There are two kidneys, each located behind the abdominal organs, against the muscles of the back near the spinal column, and protected somewhat by the ribs. This region is referred to as the *costovertebral angle* (*CVA*). The kidneys are surrounded by a cushion of fat. The kidneys are bean-shaped and are about 5 inches long and 2 inches wide in the adult. The kidneys are made up of many microscopic-sized *nephrons,* which filter materials from the blood. This process results in the formation of waste material known as *urine.* Urine is collected in the basin (pelvis) of the kidney and then drains into the ureters.

◆ **URETERS:** Each kidney has a tube to carry urine to the bladder. Each tube is pencil-thin and about 10 inches long. The term *flank* refers to the body lateral and posterior area between the bottom ribs and the hip bones. The anatomical region where the ureters and bladder meet is known as the *ureterovesical junction.*

◆ **BLADDER:** The urinary bladder is a hollow cavity, anterior to the rectum, and low in the pelvic region (*suprapubic*). The urge to urinate (*void*) occurs when the bladder contains about one-half cup of urine, but the bladder has great stretching ability.

◆ **URETHRA:** The tube carrying urine to the outside is the urethra. In the female, this is only about 2 inches long; in the male, it is about 10 inches long as it travels the length of the penis. The male urethra is surrounded by a mass of tissue just below the bladder called the *prostate.* The urethra ends at the *meatus* (orifice), or opening to the outside of the body.

◆ CLINICAL ASSESSMENT

The examiner assesses symptoms relating to urination, hypertension, diabetes, systemic infections, and medications. Examination includes observation of hydration, overall appearance of the body, skin color and turgor, and edema.

Intake and output (*I&O*) is an important consideration in many disease conditions. *Intake* refers to the amount of fluid taken into the body (ingested or parenterally). *Output* refers to the amount of urine, other drainage (nasogastric suction and wound drains), vomitus, and diarrhea expelled from the body. The physician also allows for a certain percentage of loss through respiration and perspiration.

◆ SYMPTOMS AND DISEASE CONDITIONS

Practice word recognition and pronunciation; then spell each term.

anuria	(an-yū´rē-ă)	absence of urine
bacteriuria	(bak-tēr-ē-ū´rē-ă)	bacteria in urine
benign prostatic hypertrophy (BPH)	(bē-nīn´ pros-tat´ik hī-per´trō-fē)	overgrowth of prostatic tissue (not malignant)
calculus [plural calculi]	(kal´kyū-lŭs)	stone
colic	(kol´ik)	spasmodic pain, sharp in nature
cystitis	(sis-tī´tis)	inflammation of bladder
dribbling	(dri´bling)	falling in drops involuntarily

dysuria	(dis-yū´rē-ă)	difficulty or painful urination
edema	(e-dē´mă)	excess fluid in tissues
efflux	(ēf-luks´)	something flowing out
frequency	(frē´kwen-sē)	something that happens at short intervals, as urination
glomerulonephritis	(glō-măr´yū-lō-nef-rī´tis)	inflammation of the filtering mechanism within kidney
hematuria	(hē-mă-tū´rē-ă)	blood in urine
hesitancy	(hez´i-tăn-sē)	involuntary delay in starting the urinary stream
hydronephrosis	(hī´drō-ne-frō´sis)	dilation of kidneys due to obstruction in flow of urine
hypertension	(hī´per-ten´shŭn)	high blood pressure
incontinence	(in-kon´ti-nens)	inability to control urination
stress incontinence		involuntarily expelling of urine during coughing, sneezing, laughing, etc.
lethargy	(leth´ar-jē)	unconsciousness from which one can be aroused but not without relapses
nephrolithiasis	(nef´rō-li-thī´ă-sis)	the condition of having a kidney stone
nocturia	(nok-tū´rē-ă)	urination at night
oliguria	(ol-i-gū´rē-ă)	scanty urination
proteinuria	(prō-tē-nū´rē-ă)	protein in urine
pyelonephritis	(pī´ĕ-lō-ne-frī´tis)	inflammation of kidney
pyuria	(pī-yū´rē-ă)	pus in urine
reflux	(rē´flŭks)	backflow of urine
residual urine	(rē-zid´yū-ăl)	urine left in bladder after urination
stenosis	(ste-nō´sis)	narrowing
trabeculation	(tră-bek´yū-lā´shŭn)	forming support by means of bundles of fibers
ureteritis	(yū-rē-ter-ī´tis)	inflammation of ureter
ureterolithiasis	(yū-rē´ter-ō-li-thī´ă-sis)	stone in ureter
urethritis	(yū-rē-thrī´tis)	inflammation of urethra
urgency	(er´jen-sē)	desire to void immediately
urinary tract infection (UTI)		infection of urinary tract, not including kidneys

◆ LABORATORY TESTS

Blood tests for kidney function include alkaline phosphatase, blood urea nitrogen (BUN), and creatinine.

urine culture (UC) and sensitivity	(kŭl´chŭr)	allowing a urine specimen to "grow" to identify an organism and then testing medications against that organism to identify one that "kills" it
urinalysis (UA)	(yū-ri-nal´i-sis)	examination of urine
clean-catch specimen/ midstream		urinary meatus cleansed prior to obtaining specimen or the specimen obtained "midstream"
24-hour urinalysis		collecting all urine voided over 24-hour period

URINALYSIS: A great deal of information can be obtained through the following analysis of urine:

- *Color and clarity*: Color should be clear. It can vary from almost colorless to dark yellow to tea-colored if it contains blood.

- *Specific gravity*: This is normally 1.006 to 1.030. The *pH* indicates acidity or alkalinity, varying from 4.6 to 8.0.

Urine is tested by dipstick (*Clinistix*) and should be negative for *glucose* and *ketones* but may be positive in the diabetic person. Urine that is positive for *protein* or *nitrites* may indicate kidney disease or a heart condition.

Urine is analyzed microscopically. It can normally contain 2 to 5 *red blood cells* (RBCs) per high-powered field (hpf) and less than 7 *white blood cells* (WBCs). More indicate an infection. Other abnormal findings in the urine include *crystals, casts*, and *bacteria*. *Epithelial* cells may be found in urine. *Pus* indicates an infection in the urine. One of the common bacteria found in urine culture is *E. coli* (Escherichia).

◆ X-RAY PROCEDURES

intravenous pyelogram (IVP)	(in´tră-vē´nŭs pī´el-ō-gram)	intravenous administration of dye (*contrast medium*) and subsequent X rays (*radiographs*) to see the dye travel through the urinary tract, especially noting the kidneys, ureters, and bladder
plain film of abdomen: kidney, ureter, bladder (KUB)		X ray without the use of a dye; sometimes called a "scout film"
ultrasound	(ŭl´tră-sownd)	imaging using sound waves to detect liquid or solid mass or tissue
voiding cystourethrogram (VCUG)	(sis-tō-yū-reth´rō-gram)	introducing a dye into bladder and subsequent X rays of bladder as well as urethra as patient voids

◆ MEDICAL PROCEDURES

catheterization	(kath´ĕ-ter-ī-zā´shŭn)	insertion of tube for withdrawal of urine
dialysis	(dī-al´i-sis)	artificial means of purifying blood when kidneys are not functioning
dilation or dilatation	(dī-lā´shŭn) (dīl ă tā´shŭn)	stretching

◆ SURGICAL PROCEDURES

cystoscopy	(sis-tos´kō-pē)	visual examination of the inside of the bladder
lithotripsy	(lith´ō-trip-sē)	sound waves or surgical crushing of stones
nephrectomy	(ne-frek´tō-mē)	removal of kidney
nephrolithotomy	(nef´rō-li-thot´ō-mē)	incision into kidney for removal of stones

| transurethral resection of prostate (TUR; TURP) | (trans-yū-rē´thrăl) | entering the urethra for removal of prostate |

◆ MEDICATIONS

The sulfa medications are drugs of choice for infections of the urinary system. Other medications for urinary diseases include the antibiotics, antihypertensives, antispasmodics, and analgesics.

amoxicillin	(ă-mok-si-sil´in)	antibiotic
Bactrim DS (double strength)	(bak´trim)	antibiotic
Compazine	(komp´ă-zēn)	antiemetic
Keflex	(kĕf´lĕx)	antibiotic
Macrodantin	(mak´rō-dan´tin)	antibiotic
morphine sulfate (MS)	(mōr´fēn sŭl´făt)	narcotic analgesic
Percocet	(per-kō´set)	narcotic analgesic
potassium chloride	(pō-tas´ē-ŭm klōr´īd)	mineral
Pyridium	(pī-rid´ē-ŭm)	analgesic
Septra or Septra DS (double strength)	(sep´tră)	antibiotic

A common IV solution is 5% dextrose (D5) in water or normal saline (salt). It can be prepared in 1000 cubic centimeter (one liter) amount.

◆ MISCELLANEOUS TERMS

accumulation	(a-kum´yū-lā-shŭn)	collection
cerebral palsy	(ser´ĕ-brăl pawl´zē)	spasms or paralysis due to lesion of brain, usually suffered at birth
configuration	(kon-fig-yū-rā´shŭn)	arrangement or form
contour	(kon´tūr)	outline
dorsolithotomy position	(dōr-sō-li-thot´-ō-mē)	lying on the back
extravasation	(eks-trav´ā-sā´shŭn)	escape from normal containment
hyperplasia	(hī-per-plā´zē-ă)	increase in number of cells
intubation	(in-tū-bā´shŭn)	insertion of a tube
irritative	(ir-i-tā´tiv)	inflamed
lumbosacral	(lŭm´bō-sā´krăl)	relating to vertebral region in lower back adjacent to sacrum (between hip bones)
suppository	(sŭ-poz´i-tōr-ē)	medication given rectally

◆ Catheters are measured in sizes such as French Number 24, transcribed as #24 Fr. or #24 French.

You are now ready to transcribe Tape 7.

The dictation for this chapter is by Dr. Lee W. Kim.

Remember to identify each report properly in the upper right-hand corner.

```
                        Chapter 7, Item 1
                         Student's name
                          Current date
```

TRANSCRIPTION CHECKOFF SHEET
by Patient

DOCTOR DICTATING: Lee W. Kim, M.D.

TYPE OF DICTATION: Chart notes, history and physical, X-ray reports, and procedure notes

DATE OF TRANSCRIPTION: April 17, 19--

WS- 100
T-

Item Number	Patient	Date Started	Date Completed	Grade/ Number of Errors
1	Lia Yen			
2	Sarah Adair			
3	Adella Nash			
4	Sharon Tanaka			
5	Quentin Thorne			
6	Betty Nikolai			
7	Luisa Enright			
8	Eugene Ewards			
9	Juan Verdez			
10	Carlos Hermanez			
11	Mara Kazer			
12	Anita Stokes			
13	Mitchell LaBash			
14	June Kvamme			
15	Jonathan Nissen			
16	Herald Boswellski			
17	Lee Kwan			

THE REPRODUCTIVE SYSTEM

8

◆ REPRODUCTIVE SYSTEM FUNCTION AND COMPONENTS

The anatomical structures of males and females are different. However, each system consists of sex glands (gonads), passageways, and accessory structures. Hormones from the pituitary gland influence functions of this system. The reproductive system has the following functions: reproduction, production of hormones, and sexual gratification.

Organs of the Male

The male reproductive system is shown in Figure 8.1. The *scrotum* is the sac that contains and maintains the temperature of the two *testes* (testicles), which produce *sperm* and the hormone *testosterone*. Testosterone is essential

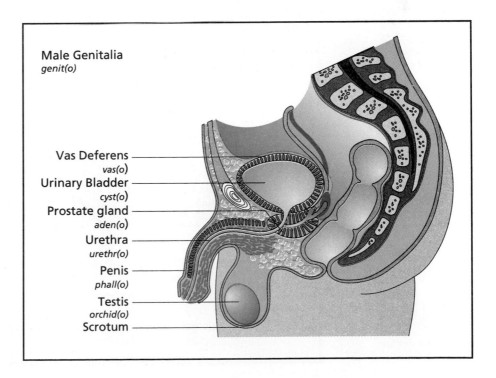

Male Genitalia
genit(o)

Vas Deferens
vas(o)
Urinary Bladder
cyst(o)
Prostate gland
aden(o)
Urethra
urethr(o)
Penis
phall(o)
Testis
orchid(o)
Scrotum

Figure 8.1 The Male
Reproductive System

for development of secondary male characteristics and an increase in skeletal muscle mass. Sperm is stored in the *epididymis* of the testis before entering the *vas deferens,* the muscular tube leading through the *inguinal canal* in the *groin* where the leg meets the body, into the pelvic cavity.

The vas with its accompanying blood vessels and nerves is called the *spermatic cord*. The vas travels through the prostate gland, which surrounds the urethra just below the bladder. Fluid is secreted from the prostate and is added to the *semen* where it aids in increasing the motility of the sperm and in neutralizing the acidity of urine. The vas joins the *urethra,* located within the *penis* (*phallus*). The end (head) of the penis (referred to as *glans penis*) is covered by the *foreskin* (*prepuce*).

The scrotum and penis are the male *external genitalia*. Accessory structures include the *seminal vesicles* and *bulbourethral glands*, which add alkaline fluid to the semen.

Organs of the Female

The two *ovaries* are located in the pelvic cavity (pelvis) on either side of the uterus and are anchored to the side of the uterus by ligaments. The ovaries produce eggs for reproduction and the hormones *estrogen* and *progesterone*. Estrogen is essential for development of female characteristics, including *menstruation,* or *menses*. Progesterone influences the preparation of the endometrial lining of the uterus and the maintenance of a pregnancy.

Several pituitary hormones affect release of the egg from the ovary (*ovulation*), as well as the phases of the menstrual cycle. The *uterine* (*fallopian*) tubes are attached to the right and left sides of the *uterus* near the ovaries. They open into the uterus located between the bladder and the rectum. The ovaries and the tubes are referred to as the *adnexa* (adnexum, singular). The *myometrium* is the muscular layer of the uterus, and the *endometrium* is the inner layer that is shed during the menses. The lower necklike portion of the uterus is the *cervix,* from which the Papanicolaou (*Pap*) smear is taken.

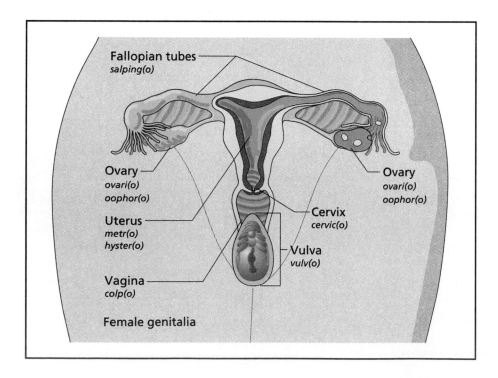

Figure 8.2 The Female Reproductive System

The *cervical os* opens into the *vagina,* which is lined with mucous membrane arranged in many folds called *rugae.* The upper region of the vagina, surrounding the cervix, is known as the *cul-de-sac.* The muscular vagina extends from the uterus to the *vulva* (*external genitalia*).

External genitalia include the *mons pubis* (the fat pad anterior to the symphysis pubis bone), the *labia minora* and *majora* (folds of skin and tissue covering the vaginal opening), and the *clitoris* (a small mass of erectile tissue at the apex of the labia). Accessory structures of the female reproductive system include the *Bartholin, Skene's,* and *urethral glands* (abbreviated as *BSU*) and the *hymen.*

Mammary Glands

Mammary glands or *breasts* are located anterior to the pectoralis major chest muscle between the second and sixth ribs, lateral to the *sternum* (breast bone), and extend to the *axilla* (armpit). The breasts are composed of *adipose tissue* (fat), lobes of glandular tissues, and the excretory ducts. The *nipples,* at about the fifth rib, contain the openings of the milk ducts. Surrounding the nipples is a circular area of pigmented skin called the *areola.* Breast development begins at puberty in the female and is influenced by hormonal function.

◆ CLINICAL ASSESSMENT

The prostate is examined digitally through the rectum to determine size, shape, and consistency. The female internal genitalia are examined with the use of a speculum. The bimanual examination refers to the use of both hands, one hand on the lower abdomen while the examiner's finger pushes internally. This examination determines uterine and adnexal size and position, as well as tenderness.

◆ SYMPTOMS AND DISEASE CONDITIONS

Practice word recognition and pronunciation; then spell each term.

AIDS		acquired immunodeficiency syndrome
cancer	(kan´ser)	malignant growth
cervicitis	(ser-vi-sī´tis)	inflammation of mucosa of cervix
Chlamydia	(kla-mid´ē-ă)	type of venereal disease
cystic breast disease	(sis´tik)	formation of fluid or semisolid sac of breast tissue
cystocele	(sis´tō-sēl)	herniation of bladder into vaginal wall
dysmenorrhea	(dis-men-ŏr-ē´ă)	menstrual cramps
dysplasia	(dis-plā´zē-ă)	abnormal tissue development
endometriosis	(en´dō-mē-trē-ō´sis)	formation of endometrial tissue outside the uterus, in the pelvic cavity
epididymitis	(ep-i-did-i-mī´tis)	inflammation of epididymis
erosion	(ē-rō´zhŭn)	wearing away
eversion	(ē-ver´zhŭn)	turning outward
gonorrhea (GC)	(gon-ō-rē´ă)	type of venereal disease
gynecomastia	(gī´nō-kō-mas´tē-ă)	excessive breast development in male
herpes	(her´pēz)	type of venereal disease
human Papilloma virus (HPV)	(pap-i-lō´mă)	type of venereal disease

induration	(in-dū-rā´shŭn)	pulling inward, swelling
inguinal	(ing´gwi-năl)	relating to the groin
mastalgia	(mas-tal´jē-ă)	breast pain
menopause	(men´ō-pawz)	cessation of menses
menorrhagia	(men-ō-rā´jē-ă)	excessive bleeding at time of period
metrorrhagia	(mē-trō-rā´jē-ă)	bleeding between periods
orange-peel appearance (peau d'orange)	(pō-dō-rahnj´)	puckered appearance to skin of breast
orchitis	(ōr-kī´tis)	inflammation of testis
osteoporosis	(os´tē-ō-pō-rō´sis)	reduction in bone density
pelvic inflammatory disease (PID)		inflammation of uterus, tubes, and ovaries
premenstrual syndrome (PMS)		group of symptoms occurring before the menstrual period
prolapse of uterus	(prō-laps´)	displacement of uterus into vagina
pruritus	(prū-rī´tŭs)	itching
rectocele	(rek´tō-sēl)	herniation of rectum into vaginal wall
sexually transmitted diseases (STDs)		
torsion	(tōr´shŭn)	twisting
Trichomonas	(trik-o-mō´nas)	parasitic infection
vaginosis	(vaj´i-nō´sis)	bacterial infection of vagina

◆ LABORATORY PROCEDURES

Blood is tested for human immunodeficiency virus (HIV).
Penile and vaginal secretions may be tested for the following:

Chlamydia	(kla-mid´ē-ă)
Gonococcus (GC)	(gon-ō-kok´ŭs)
herpesvirus	(her´pēz-vī´rŭs)
Human immunodeficiency virus (HIV)	
human Papillomavirus (HPV)	(pap-i-lō´mă-vī-rŭs)
KOH staining (a technique)	
wet prep/mount (a technique)	

◆ X-RAY PROCEDURES

mammogram	(mam´ō-gram)	breast X ray

◆ MEDICAL PROCEDURES

breast self-exam		
colposcopy	(kol-pos´kŏ-pē)	vaginal and cervical examination with endoscope
cryotherapy	(krī-ō-thăr´ă-pē)	use of cold for treatment
loop electrosurgical excision procedure (LEEP)		removal of tissue from the cervix
Pap smear		test for cervical cancer
Sitz bath	(sitz)	sitting and soaking area from tailbone to lower abdomen in a tub of warm water
testicular self-exam		

◆ SURGICAL PROCEDURES

circumcision	(ser-kŭm-sizh´ŭn)	removal of penile foreskin
cystorrhaphy	(sis-tōr´ă-fē)	suturing of urinary bladder
dilatation & curettage (D&C)	(dil-ă-tā´shŭn and kyū-rĕ-tahzh´)	stretching and scraping uterine cavity
endocervical curettage	(en´dō-ser´vi-kăl kyū-rĕ-tahzh´)	scraping within cervix
hysterectomy	(his-ter-ek´tō-mē)	removal of uterus
laparoscopy	(lap-ă-ros´kō-pē)	viewing internal abdominal organs with endoscope
lumpectomy	(lŭm-pek´tō-mē)	removal of lump from breast
mastectomy	(mas-tek´tō-mē)	excision of breast
oophorosalpingectomy	(ō-of´ōr-ō-sal-pin-jek´tō-mē)	removal of ovary and tube
uterine suspension	(yū´ter-in)	tightening structures that hold uterus in place
vasectomy	(va-sek´tō-mē)	removal of segment of vas deferens

◆ MEDICATIONS

doxycycline	(dok-sē-sī´klēn)	antibiotic
Estraderm	(s´tra-derm)	hormone
Motrin	(mō´trin)	NSAID, analgesic, antipyretic
Norplant	(nōr´plant)	contraceptive
tamoxifen	(tă-mok´si-fen)	antineoplastic

◆ MISCELLANEOUS TERMS

incarceration	(in-kar´ser-ā-shŭn)	being trapped
Jackson-Pratt drain	(jak´son-prat)	tube used for wound drainage
marginated	(mar´ji-nāt-ed)	specific outline that occurs in early inflammation
pendulous	(pen´dū-lŭs)	hanging freely
squamous atypia	(skwā´mŭs ā-tip´ē-ă)	not the usual platelike cells
Steri-strips	(ster´ē)	trade name for specific adhesive bandage
strangulation	(strang´gyū-lā´shŭn)	constriction of blood flow
transillumination	(trans-i-lū´mi-nā´shŭn)	passing a strong light through
vertigo	(ver´ti-gō)	dizziness

- There is no nipple dimpling, discharge, or mass.

- The prostate is smooth and nontender.

- The prostate is 2+ and boggy.

- There was no costovertebral angle (CVA) tenderness.

You are now ready to transcribe Tape 8.

The dictation for this chapter is by Dr. Debra Litman.

Remember to identify each report properly in the upper right-hand corner.

```
                          Chapter 8, Item 1
                            Student's name
                            Current date
```

After the Chapter 8 transcription has been corrected and returned to you for review, you are ready to take Transcription Test 3. Obtain the test tape from your instructor.

TRANSCRIPTION CHECKOFF SHEET
by Patient

DOCTOR DICTATING: Debra Litman, M.D.

TYPE OF DICTATION: Chart notes, procedure notes, and X-ray report

DATE OF TRANSCRIPTION: April 19, 19--

Item Number	Patient	Date Started	Date Completed	Grade/ Number of Errors
1	Richard Kaplan			
2	Jared Hoffmeier			
3	Suzette Meyers			
4	Donna Hooley			
5	Paulo Hernandez			
6	Soon Lee Yim			
7	Shelley Ellis			
8	Chi Hyatt			
9	Rodney Armstrong			
10	Ann Sankaaran			
11.	Leah Ahmann			
12.	Sandra Pascoe			
13.	Tasha Sprague			

9 ◆ THE MUSCULOSKELETAL SYSTEM

◆ MUSCULOSKELETAL SYSTEM FUNCTION AND COMPONENTS

The musculoskeletal system includes the bones and muscles with their attached ligaments and tendons. The functioning of bones and muscles is interrelated with the endocrine system, which produces hormones that affect their growth, and with the nervous system, which sends impulses that affect their movement. An adequate blood supply is essential to the functioning of muscles and bones.

The bones have the following functions:

- ◆ **FRAMEWORK:** The muscles are attached to the bones to provide the framework of the body.

- ◆ **PROTECTION:** The bones provide protection for the internal organs.

- ◆ **MOVEMENT:** The muscles provide movement of the body.

- ◆ **STORAGE OF CALCIUM:** Calcium is needed by bones, teeth, nerves, and other structures in order to function properly.

- ◆ **PRODUCTION OF BLOOD CELLS:** Red and white blood cells are formed in the bone marrow.

Bones

Bones are covered with a tough membrane called the *periosteum*. The ends of the bones are covered with *cartilage*.

The connection of two or more bones is called a *joint* or an *articulation*. Some joints, especially those that move a lot, contain a sac filled with *synovial fluid,* which allows for ease in movement. A bursa is a fluid-filled sac found in areas that are subject to friction (that is, where a tendon passes over a bone). Joints may be identified by using the names of the connecting bones and/or their location, such as temporomandibular joint, sacroiliac joint, costochondral junction, proximal interphalangeal joint (PIP), metacarpophalangeal joint (MCP), and so forth.

Joints also have a tough band of tissue, a *ligament,* that connects bone to bone and reinforces the joint. A common group of ligaments are the collaterals in the knee.

Tendons attach bones to muscles. An example is the Achilles tendon in the heel region.

Bones have many landmarks, only a few of which are identified here:

acromion	(ă-krō′mē-on)	bony projection forming part of shoulder joint
condyle	(kon′dīl)	bulge (on a bone)
epiphysis	(e-pif′i-sis)	end, or growing region, of a long bone
fontanel	(fon′tă-nel′)	"soft spot" or joint in skull (cranium) of infants before bones have fused
head		upper portion of arm and leg bones
lamina	(lam′i-nă)	a region of vertebra
malleolus	(ma-lē′ō-lŭs)	projection on either side of
(plural, malleoli)	(ma-lē′ō-lī)	lower leg (the ankle)
sciatic notch	(sī-at′ik)	depression in ischial bone
shaft	(shaft)	midportion of a long bone
sinus	(sī′nŭs)	air pocket in bone to make bone lighter
styloid	(stī′loyd)	sharp projection
trochanter	(trō-kan′ter)	big bulge on upper leg bone
tuberosity	(tū′ber-os′i-tē)	big bulge or knob

Using standard references, enter the appropriate number from Figure 9.1 next to the bone shown below:

_____ calcaneus (kal-kā′nē-ŭs)

_____ carpals (kar′păls)

_____ cervical vertebra (ser′vi-kăl ver′tĕ-bră)

_____ clavicle (klav′i-kl)

_____ coccyx (kok′siks)

_____ cranium (krā′nē-ŭm)

_____ femur (fē′mŭr)

_____ fibula (fib′yū-lă)

_____ humerus (hyū′mer-ŭs)

_____ ilium (il′ē-ŭm)

_____ lumbar vertebra (lŭm′bar ver′tĕ-bră)

_____ metacarpals (met′ă-kar′păls)

_____ metatarsals (met′ă-tar′săls)

_____ patella (pa-tel′ă)

_____ phalanges (fă-lan′jēz)

_____ radius (rā′dē-ŭs)

_____ ribs (ribs)

_____ sacrum (sā′krŭm)

_____ scapula (skap′yū-lă)

_____ sternum (ster′num)

_____ tarsals (tar′săls)

_____ thoracic vertebra   (thō-ras´ik ver´tĕ-bră)

_____ tibia   (tib´ē-ă)

_____ ulna   (ŭl´nă)

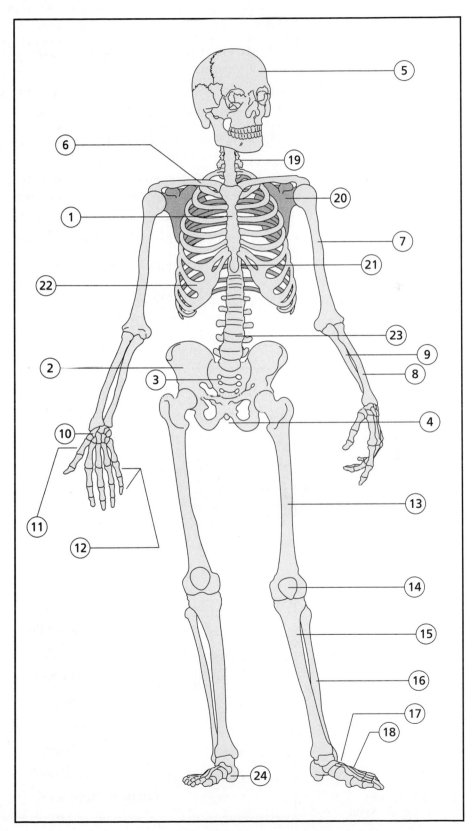

Figure 9.1 Major Bones of the Body

Muscles

Muscles attach to bones of the skeleton, and they make up the walls of internal organs including the heart. The nervous system is involved with stimulation of the muscles to initiate muscle function. There are more than 600 muscles in the body. This chapter concentrates on the skeletal muscles.

Muscles have the following functions:

◆ **MOVEMENT:** This includes movement of the bones as well as activity of the internal organs.

◆ **MAINTENANCE OF POSTURE:** This involves controlling muscles to keep the body in normal functioning positions.

◆ **HEAT PRODUCTION:** This entails producing body heat from the movement of the skeletal muscles.

Bones and muscles work together to produce movement of body parts. They frequently work in pairs. As shown in Figure 9.2, these are some of the common joint movements:

◆ **ABDUCTION** moves away from the body.

◆ **ADDUCTION** moves toward the midline of the body.

◆ **CIRCUMDUCTION** (of the shoulders and hips) allows movement in a circle.

◆ **EXTENSION** increases the size of an angle.

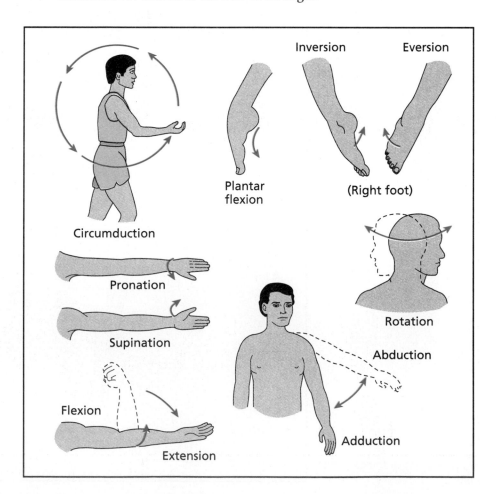

Figure 9.2 Common Movements of the Joints

◆ **FLEXION** decreases the size of an angle.

◆ **EVERSION** turns outward.

◆ **INVERSION** turns inward.

◆ **PRONATION** (of the forearm) places the palm down.

◆ **SUPINATION** (of the forearm) places the palm up.

◆ **ROTATION** moves the head from side to side.

Using standard references, enter the appropriate number from Figure 9.3 next to the muscles shown below:

_____ abdominal	_____ inner upper arm
_____ anterior thigh	_____ lower back
_____ anterior lower leg	_____ major neck muscle

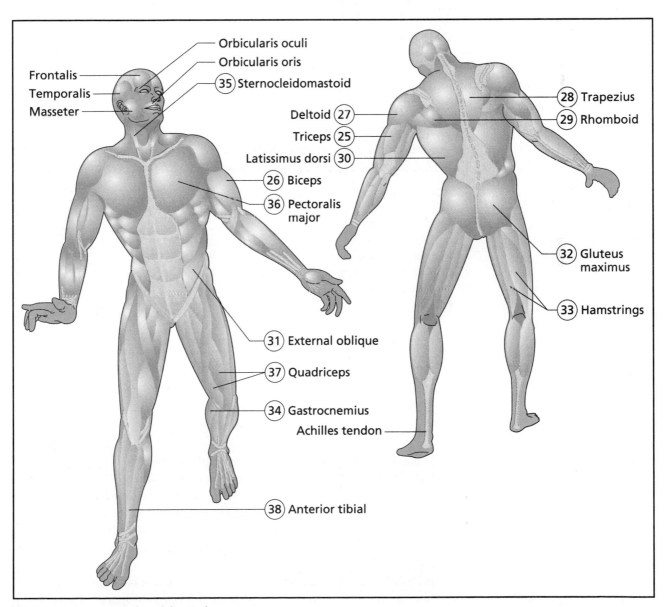

Figure 9.3 Major Muscles of the Body

_____	between shoulder blades	_____	outer upper arm
_____	buttocks	_____	posterior thigh
_____	calf	_____	shoulder cap
_____	chest	_____	upper back, shoulder-to-shoulder and across vertebrae

◆ CLINICAL ASSESSMENT

The examiner observes this system for muscle functioning: complete range of motion (ROM) of joints, muscle strength (dictated as five over five—5/5—or intact), bulk, and tone.

The nervous system works with the musculoskeletal system; thus associated functions are tested. These include deep tendon reflex testing (DTRs) of knee, ankle, patella, triceps, and biceps. Radial and ulnar jerks are also evaluated.

Circulation is observed, since it is often compromised during injury when there is swelling and/or broken blood vessels.

◆ MANEUVERS, SIGNS, AND TESTS

Following is a list of maneuvers, signs, and tests that apply to the examination of the musculoskeletal system. Review a reference source for explanations. Note that some references show possession with 's; others do not use 's.

Apley grind	Phalen test
apprehension sign	range of motion (ROM)
deep tendon reflexes (DTRs)	active
drawer sign	passive
heel-and-toe walk	spring test
impingement sign	straight-leg raise test
McMurray test	Tinel's sign
Patrick's test	

◆ SYMPTOMS AND DISEASE CONDITIONS

Practice word recognition and pronunciation; then spell each term.

alignment	(ă-līn′ment)	proper position
arthritis	(ar-thrī′tis)	joint inflammation
avulsion	(ă-vŭl′shŭn)	separation
bursitis	(ber-sī′tus)	inflammation of bursa
carpal tunnel syndrome	(kar′păl)	symptoms such as pain and weakness in wrist caused by pressure on median nerve
Colles fracture	(kōl′ez)	fractured radius with displacement
costochondritis	(kos′tō-kon-drī′tis)	inflammation of cartilage between ribs
crepitus	(krep′i-tŭs)	crackling or bubbling sound or feeling
degenerative joint disease (DJD)	(dē-jen′er-ă-tiv)	deterioration of joints
dislocation	(dis′lō-kā′shŭn)	displacement; disruption of proper position
effusion	(e-fū′zhŭn)	excessive fluid in joint space

fracture	(frak´chūr)	break
gout (gouty arthritis)	(gowt)	deposits of crystals in joints
herniated (ruptured) disc	(her´nē-ā-ted)	disk that protrudes
myositis	(mī-ō-sī´tis)	inflammation of muscle
radiculopathy	(ra-dik´yū-lop´ă-thē)	disease of spinal nerve roots
strain	(strān)	muscle injury caused by overuse or improper use
tendonitis or tendinitis	(ten-dō-nī´tis or ten-di-nī´tis)	inflammation of tendon

◆ LABORATORY TEST

Serum uric acid	(ur´ik)	

◆ X-RAY PROCEDURES

C-spine		X ray of cervical spine
plain films		X rays taken to outline bones, looking for abnormalities; X rays that do not use contrast media

◆ MEDICAL PROCEDURES

cast	(kast)	application of rigid material to prevent movement
crutch	(krŭtch)	device used for support (usually under the armpit) when walking
electromyogram (EMG)	(ē-lek-trō-mī´ō-gram)	a graphic representation of muscle function that uses electrical stimulation
immobilization	(i-mō´bi-li-zā-shŭn)	prevention of movement
sling	(sling)	piece of cloth looped under arm and around shoulder and/or neck for arm support
splint	(splint)	temporary device to prevent movement of bone

◆ SURGICAL PROCEDURES

arthroscopy	(ar-thros´kŏ-pē)	visual examination of a joint using special surgical instrument
laminectomy	(lam´i-nek´tō-mē)	removal of part of a vertebra
prosthesis (joint replacement)	(pros´thē-sis)	surgical removal of worn-out structure (cartilage) and replacement with artificial mechanism

◆ MEDICATIONS

Aleve	(ă-lēv)	NSAID, analgesic
allopurinol	(al-ō-pyū´ri-nol)	antigout

Aristospan	(ă-rist´ō-span)	cortisone
(triamcinolone)	(trī-am-sin´ō-lōn)	
aspirin	(as´pi-rin)	analgesic, antipyretic
Daypro	(da´prō)	NSAID
Naprosyn	(nap´rō-sin)	analgesic, antipyretic

◆ MISCELLANEOUS TERMS

chiropractic	(kī-rō-prak´tik)	method of treating disease by manipulation of joints
gait	(gāt)	method of walking
laxity	(lak´să-tē)	looseness
neurosensory	(nūr´ō-sen´sŏ-rē)	relating to nerve sensation
neurovascular	(nūr-ō-vas´kyū-lăr)	having to do with nerve blood vessels
numbness	(nŭm´nes)	without feeling
oblique	(ob-lēk´)	in a slanted position
orthopedics	(ōr-thō-pē´diks)	branch of medicine dealing with conditions of the musculoskeletal system
pivot	(piv´ŏt)	point at which something turns or hinges

THE NERVOUS SYSTEM

10

◆ NERVOUS SYSTEM FUNCTION AND COMPONENTS

The main function of the nervous system is to control and coordinate the body's movements and functions and to receive sensory input from various parts of the body. This is accomplished by nerves' responding to stimuli. The nervous system consists of nerves, brain, spinal cord, and sense organs.

A nerve is made up of special cells (neurons) and their supporting structures. These structures act like a telephone communication or relay system, carrying impulses to and from the body parts and the brain.

Nerves are classified by their functions.

◆ **SENSORY NERVES:** These nerves carry impulses from the body to the brain or spinal cord. These impulses are known as sensations and include touch, pressure, pain, temperature, and proprioception (or position sense).

◆ **MOTOR NERVES:** The motor nerves carry impulses away from the brain or spinal cord, out to muscles and glands, and produce movement.

Components

The two main parts of the nervous system are the central nervous system and the peripheral nervous system.

Central Nervous System (CNS)

The central nervous system consists of the brain and spinal cord. The brain contains centers that control involuntary functions such as circulation, temperature regulation, respiration, and impressions from the eyes and ears. It is the processing center of consciousness, emotion, thought, memory, and reasoning.

Major structures of the brain include the following:

The *cerebrum*, which is responsible for memory, interpretation of sensations, and voluntary movement.

The *cerebellum*, which coordinates voluntary movement, posture, and equilibrium.

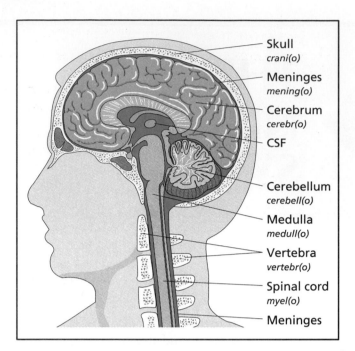

Figure 10.1 The Nervous System

The *medulla* functions as the center for respiration, blood pressure, and cardiac activity. The medulla and its accompanying structures are sometimes called the *brainstem*.

Figure 10.1 shows the major structures of the brain and the protective structures.

The spinal cord is found within the spinal column, surrounded by the vertebrae. It connects to the medulla and ends about the level of the first lumbar vertebra. The function of the spinal cord is to relay messages (*impulses*) from the body to the brain and to send messages from the brain to the body.

The brain and spinal cord are surrounded by thin membranes called the *meninges* (pia mater, arachnoid, and dura mater), which are protective structures. Within these membranes is the fluid called *cerebrospinal fluid* (CSF), which serves as a shock absorber. In Figure 10.2, a cross section illustrates the location of the cord and spinal nerves surrounded by the meninges and vertebra.

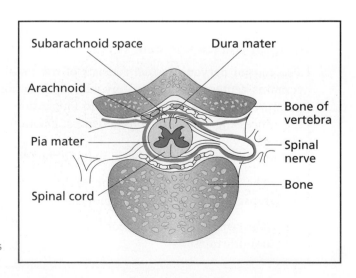

Figure 10.2 Spinal Cord Cross Section

The Peripheral Nervous System

The peripheral nervous system involves the cranial nerves (off the brain), spinal nerves (off the spinal cord), and the autonomic (automatic) nerves, which is a link between the CNS and body parts such as the skin, muscles, and internal organs. It is made of the following subdivisions:

◆ **CRANIAL NERVES:** Attached to the undersurface of the brain are the cranial nerves. There are 12 pairs (arranged on the right and the left sides of the brain). Each pair has a name and controls impulses mainly in the head and neck region.

◆ **SPINAL NERVES:** The spinal nerves are attached to the right and the left sides of the spinal cord and exit through openings between the vertebrae. There are 31 pairs, corresponding to their location. (For example, L3-4 means its location is between the third and fourth lumbar vertebrae.) The spinal nerves conduct impulses between parts of the body and the spinal cord.

◆ **AUTONOMIC NERVOUS SYSTEM:** The autonomic nervous system controls the internal organs and normal functions. It works with adrenaline in times of stress. The functions that are affected are breathing, circulation, digestion, excretion, and hormone secretion.

◆ **THE SENSE ORGANS:** Functions of the sense organs include those having to do with taste, smell, sight, hearing, and sensation. The eyes and ears are briefly discussed in this unit.

■ **THE EYES:** The eyes are located in the eye socket or *orbit,* surrounded by bone for protection. Three layers of tissue form the eyeball: the *sclera,* or "white" part of the eye; the *choroid* or middle layer containing special muscles and blood vessels; and the *retina* or inner layer that contains the cells of vision.

Use Figure 10.3 to locate the following structures within the eye:

The *conjunctiva,* a thin membrane covering the front of the eyeball and lining the eyelids.

The *cornea,* the transparent covering of the eye overlying the muscular *iris,* the colored part of the eye.

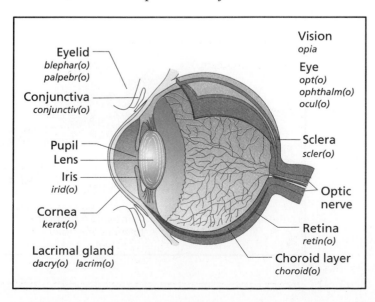

Figure 10.3 The Structures of the Eye

The *pupil*, a hole in the center of the iris which allows light to enter.

The *lens*, a transparent body that focuses light rays on the retina.

The *cranial nerve* (*optic*), which transmits the impulses to the brain for interpretation (vision).

The *lacrimal glands (tear glands)*, placed superiorly and laterally, with their ducts draining into the nose. The extraocular muscles (EOMs) move the eyes in all directions.

■ **THE EARS:** The ears are located in the temporal region of the skull. The external or visible part of the ear is the pinna. Extending inward is the *auditory canal*, which is lined with hairs. The lining secretes *cerumen* (*earwax*), which along with the hairs aids in preventing the entrance of foreign substances.

The middle ear is a tiny cavity lined with mucous membrane. The innermost part contains the *ossicles*, which vibrate with sound waves. The *tympanic membrane* (TM), or eardrum, separates the middle ear from the inner ear. The *eustachian tube* is a pathway leading from the middle ear to the throat; it functions in equalizing pressure to facilitate vibrations of the tympanic membrane. These vibrations are transmitted to the *labyrinth* (inner ear). The inner ear contains the acoustic nerve for hearing as well as structures that aid in maintaining balance.

Locate the above structures in Figure 10.4.

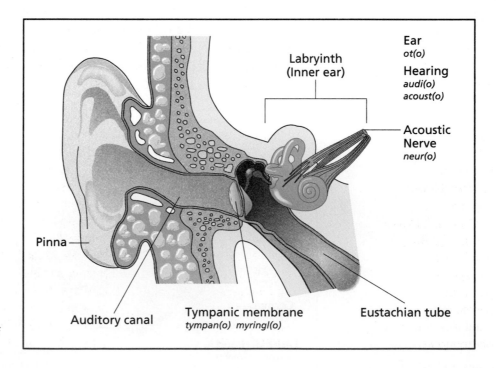

Figure 10.4 The Structures of the Ear

◆ CLINICAL ASSESSMENT

The neurologic eye exam includes the gross general notations that the pupils are equal, round, and reactive to light and accommodation (PERRLA). The funduscopic exam checks the retinae and optic discs. The extraocular movements or motions (EOMs) check the movement of eye muscles. More definitive tests may include visual fields (central and peripheral vision) and visual acuity.

The examiner tests *tactile* (touch) sensation and two-point discrimination (ability to distinguish two compass points 2 to 3 cm apart), perception of pain (*pinprick*) and temperature, joint position, vibratory sense, coordination (finger-to-nose, heel-to-shin, tandem walk), and gait.

The Romberg test examines coordination. Deep tendon reflexes (DTRs) include the biceps, triceps, brachioradial, knee and ankle jerks, and plantar reflex (Babinski's sign). The reflexes are graded on a scale of 1 to 4.

Each of the cranial nerves is tested with a specific task the patient is asked to perform (for example, shrugging the shoulders, squinting, or pursing the lips).

◆ SYMPTOMS AND DISEASE CONDITIONS

Practice word recognition and pronunciation; then spell each term.

agitation	(aj´ĕ-tā-shŭn)	moving about excitedly or disturbed
analgesia	(an-ăl-jē´zē-ă)	insensibility to pain
anesthesia	(an´es-thē´zē-ă)	loss of sensation
aphasia	(ă-fā´zē-ă)	impaired speech
apraxia	(ă-prak´sē-ă)	inability to perform voluntary movement
ataxia	(ă-tak´sē-ă)	inability to coordinate voluntary muscles for movement
cataract	(kat´ă-rakt)	loss of transparency of eye lens
cerebrovascular accident (CVA)	(ser´ĕ-brō-vas´kyū-lăr)	stroke
concussion	(kon-kŭsh´ŭn)	violent jarring of brain
conjunctivitis	(kon-jŭnk-ti-vī´tis)	inflammation of conjunctiva
convulsion	(kon-vŭl´shŭn)	seizure
epilepsy	(ep´i-lep´sē)	excessive electrical activity in brain
focal	(fō´kăl)	located in one area; localized
ganglion	(gang´glē-on)	cystlike swelling
glaucoma	(glaw-kō´mă)	disease characterized by increased intraocular pressure
herpes zoster	(her´pēz zos´ter)	shingles
ischemia	(is-kē´mē-ă)	decreased blood supply
labyrinthitis	(lab´ĭ-rin-thī´tis)	inflammation in inner ear
lightheadedness		dizziness
migraine	(mī´grān)	severe headache
multiple sclerosis	(mŭl´ti-pl sklĕ-rō´sis)	condition affecting the spinal cord
nuchal rigidity	(nū´kăl)	stiff neck
numbness	(nŭm´nes)	absence of feeling
nystagmus	(nis-tag´mŭs)	jerking eye movement
paralysis	(pă-ral´i-sis)	loss of voluntary movement
paresthesia	(par-es-thē´zē-ă)	abnormal sensation; tingling
Parkinson's disease	(par´kin-sonz)	shaking or trembling palsy
photophobia	(fō-tō-fō´bē-ă)	sensitivity to light

ptosis	(tō´sis)	downward organ displacement
sciatica	(sī-at´i-kă)	pain in lower back and hip radiating down posterior thigh
sty; stye	(stī)	inflammation of oil gland of eyelid
syncope	(sin´kŏ-pē)	fainting
tic	(tik)	twitch
transient ischemic attack (TIA)	(trans´shĕnt is-kē´mik)	short-term interruption of blood supply to brain; light stroke
vertigo	(ver´ti-gō)	feeling as if room is spinning; dizziness

◆ MEDICAL PROCEDURES

carotid ultrasound	(ka-rot´id)	image showing blood flow through carotid arteries
electroencephalogram (EEG)	(ē-lek´trō-en-sef´ă-lō-gram)	record of brain activity
tympanogram	(tim´pă-nō-gram)	record of tympanic membranes

◆ MEDICATIONS

amitriptyline	(am-i-trip´ti-lēn)	antidepressant
Antivert	(ant´i-vert)	antivertigo
Biaxin	(bī-ak´sin)	antibiotic
Cafergot	(kaf´er-got)	vasoconstrictor
Fluorescein	(flūr-es´ē-in)	dye indicator for corneal trauma
Gantrisin	(gan´tri-sin)	antibiotic
Garamycin	(gar-ă-mī´sin)	antibiotic
Imitrex	(im´i-trex)	antimigraine
Midrin	(mid´rin)	analgesic
phenobarbital	(fē-nō-bar´bi-tahl)	sedative
Pontocaine	(pont´ō-kān)	anesthetic
sodium SULAMYD	(sul´ă-mid)	bacteriostatic
sulfacetamide	(sŭl-fă-set´ă-mīd)	bacteriostatic
Tobrex	(tō´brex)	antibiotic
Valium	(val´ē-ŭm)	antianxiety
Visine	(vī-sēn´)	ocular decongestant

◆ MISCELLANEOUS TERMS

achiness	(āk´ē-ness)	feeling of pain
blepharitis	(blef´a-rī-tis)	inflammation of eyelid
debilitated	(dĕ-bil´i-tāt-ed)	extremely weakened
gaze	(gāz)	looking steadily
hertz (Hz)	(hertz´)	unit of frequency
ophthalmology	(of-thal-mol´ō-jē)	branch of medicine concerned with diagnosis and treatment of eye diseases
otolarnygology	(o´to-lar-ing-gol´o-jē)	branch of medicine concerned with diagnosis and treatment of ears, nose, and throat
psychiatry	(sī-kī´ă-trē)	branch of medicine concerned with diagnosis and treatment of mental disorders

Hints for Transcription

Before you begin the transcription for this chapter, review the following:

◆ Roman numerals, which are generally used to describe the twelve cranial nerves.

- Cranial Nerves II-XII are grossly intact.
  Note: Cranial Nerve I is the olfactory for smell and is generally not tested, unless it is an extensive exam of all the cranial nerves.

◆ The grading of reflexes. A reflex of 0 indicates no response; 1+, low normal; 2+, average or normal; 3+, brisker than normal; and 4+ is indicative of a disease process.

◆ The measuring of visual acuity. Visual acuity is measured at 20 feet, thus the first number is always 20; the second number varies according to the vision as measured on a standard scale. Therefore, 20/20 is considered normal; 20/200 indicates the ability to see only the largest letter on the vision chart.

You are now ready to transcribe Tape 10.

The dictation for this chapter is by Dr. Lynn Solinski.

Remember to identify each report properly in the upper right-hand corner.

```
                    Chapter 10, Item 1
                       Student's name
                        Current date
```

After the Chapter 10 transcription has been corrected and returned to you for review, you are ready to take Transcription Test 4. Obtain the test tape from your instructor.

TRANSCRIPTION CHECKOFF SHEET
by Patient

DOCTOR DICTATING: Lynn Solinski, M.D.

TYPE OF DICTATION: Chart notes, letter, and history and physical

DATE OF TRANSCRIPTION: April 24, 19--

Item Number	Patient	Date Started	Date Completed	Grade/ Number of Errors
1	Julia Liberstrom			
2	Andrew Brewster			
3	Marsha Dahlheimer			
4	Jared Carlos			
5	Donovan Westrum			
6	Arnold Stronovich			
7	Lia Jen Chambers			
8	Richard Lighttree			
9	~~Healther~~ Sherman *Heather*			
10	Tamara Neubauer			
11	Timothy Blesi			

APPENDIX A
REFERENCES

◆ ABBREVIATION BOOKS

Sloane, Sheila B. *Medical Abbreviations and Eponyms.* W. B. Saunders Company, Philadelphia, 1985.
Sloane, Sheila B. *The Medical Word Book.* W. B. Saunders Company, Philadelphia, 1991.
Stedman's Abbreviations, Acronyms and Symbols. Williams & Wilkins, Baltimore, 1992.

◆ DICTIONARIES

English Dictionary:
Webster's Third New International Dictionary, Unabridged. Merriam-Webster, Inc., Springfield, Massachusetts, 1993.

Medical Dictionaries:
Dorland's Illustrated Medical Dictionary. W. B. Saunders Company, Philadelphia, 1994.
Miller-Keane Encyclopedia & Dictionary of Medicine, Nursing & Allied Health. W. B. Saunders Company, Philadelphia, 1992.
Stedman's Medical Dictionary. Williams & Wilkins, Baltimore, 1995.

◆ DRUG BOOKS

Billups, Norman F. *American Drug Index.* J. B. Lippincott, Philadelphia, (annual publication).
Drake, Ellen, and Randy Drake. *Saunders Pharmaceutical Word Book.* W. B. Saunders Company, Philadelphia, (annual update).
Physicians' Desk Reference (PDR). Medical Economics, Oradell, New Jersey (annual publication).
Physicians' Desk Reference for Nonprescription Drugs. Medical Economics, Oradell, New Jersey (annual publication).

◆ GENERAL MEDICINE

Dorland's Electronic Medical Speller for WordPerfect. W. B. Saunders Company, Philadelphia, 1992.
Fisher, J. Patrick. *Basic Medical Terminology.* Bobbs-Merrill Company, Indianapolis, 1993.
Merck Manual, The. Merck Publishing Group, Inc., Rahway, New Jersey, 1992.
Sloane, Sheila B. *The Medical Word Book.* W. B. Saunders Company, Philadelphia, 1991.
Stedman's Medical Equipment Words. Williams & Wilkins, Baltimore, 1993.
Stedman's Medical Speller. Williams & Wilkins, Baltimore, 1992.

◆ GRAMMAR REVIEW/STYLE MANUAL

Diehl, Marcy O., and Marilyn T. Fordney. *Medical Transcription Guide: Do's and Don'ts.* W. B. Saunders Company, Philadelphia, 1990.
Mitchell, Carol A. *Machine Transcription.* Glencoe-McGraw-Hill, Westerville, Ohio, 1996.
Sabin, William A. *The Gregg Reference Manual.* Glencoe-Macmillan/McGraw-Hill, Westerville, Ohio, 1997.
Sloane, Sheila B., and Marilyn T. Fordney. *Saunders Manual of Medical Transcription.* W. B. Saunders Company, Philadelphia, 1993.
Tessier, Claudia, and Sally C. Pitman. *Style Guide for Medical Transcription.* American Association for Medication Transcription, Modesto, California, 1985.
Willeford, George, Jr. *Webster's New World Medical Word Finder.* Prentice-Hall, Englewood Cliffs, New Jersey, 1987.

APPENDIX B
DRUG CLASSIFICATIONS

Drugs and medicines are classified according to their use in the body. Some common classifications are shown in the following list:

analgesic	gives pain relief	contraceptive	prevents conception, or pregnancy
anesthetic	causes loss of sensation	cortisone and steroids	influence metabolism, inflammation, and physiologic stress
antacid	neutralizes acidity, especially in the GI tract		
antianxiety	relieves emotional tension	decongestant	decreases congestion or swelling in respiratory tract
antiarrhythmic	regulates irregular heart rhythm		
antibiotic	kills living microorganisms that cause infection	disinfectant	destroys bacteria on objects; not used on living tissue
anticoagulant	prevents blood clotting	diuretic	increases urine output
anticonvulsant	prevents convulsions and seizures	emetic	causes vomiting
		expectorant	aids in expelling mucus from respiratory tract
antidepressant	relieves depression		
antidiabetic	treats diabetes	glucocorticoid and corticosteroids	influence metabolism and reduce inflammation
antidiarrheal	relieves or corrects diarrhea		
antidote	counteracts or neutralizes a poison	hypolipidemic	lowers blood cholesterol
		keratolytic	assists in loosening horny layer of skin
antiemetic	reduces vomiting		
antihistamine	treats allergy symptoms	laxative	aids in having a bowel movement
antihypertensive	lowers blood pressure		
anti-inflammatory	reduces inflammation	miotic	causes pupil of eye to contract
antimicrobial	destroys microorganisms	mydriatic	causes pupil of eye to dilate
antineoplastic	treats cancers	narcotic	relieves pain or causes sleep; addictive
antipruritic	relieves itching		
antipsychotic	treats psychotic (out-of-touch-with-reality) disorders	NSAID	nonsteroidal anti-inflammatory drug
antipyretic	reduces fever	scabicide	destroys scabies
antiseptic	stops growth of microorganisms	sedative	exerts tranquilizing, soothing effect
antitussive	relieves cough	stimulant	increases activity
antivertigo	relieves dizziness	vaccine	causes resistance to specific disease
antiviral	weakens a virus		
anxiolytic	relieves anxiety	vasoconstrictor	causes blood vessels to constrict
bacteriostatic	inhibits growth of bacteria		
bronchodilator	dilates bronchial tubes	vasodilator	causes vessels to dilate
cardiotonics	affects heart action		

APPENDIX C
TROUBLESOME WORDS

Some common troublesome words are shown below indicating if they are one word, two words, hyphenated words, or confusing-alike words.

accept, except
access, assess, excess
addiction, adduction, abduction
advice, advise
(verb) affect, effect (noun)
all right
arrhythmia, erythema
arterial, arteriolar
aural, oral
auxiliary, axillary
backache
backup (n.), back up (v.)
Band-Aid
bare, bear
bedrest
bedsore
border, boarder
breakdown (n.), break down (v.)
breath, breadth
cauterization, catheterization
cease, seize
check up (v.)
checkup (n.)
cheekbone
chicken pox
chord, cord
cirrhosis, psoriasis
cite, sight, site (place)
clear-cut
coarse, course
conscience, conscious
contusion, confusion, concussion
creatine, creatinine
cul-de-sac
defuse, diffuse
diaphoresis, diuresis
die, dye
dipstick
discreet, discrete
downgoing
dysphagia, dysphasia, dysplasia

earache
eardrum
earwax
effective, affective
elicit, illicit
enteric, icteric
eyeball
eyebrow
eyedrops
eyelid
face-lift
facial, fascial
facies, feces
fecal, fetal, fatal
fee-for-service
fiberoptic
fingerbreadths
fingernail
fingertip
finger-to-nose test
flexor, flexure
follow-through (n.), follow through (v.)
follow up (v.), follow-up (n., adj.)   F/U
gait, gate
gallbladder
gallstones
hammertoe
hamstring
headache
head-tilt
heartbeat
heartburn
heatstroke
heel-to-shin test
hypocalcemia, hypokalemia
ileum (ileal), ilium (ilial)
imminent, eminent
in situ
incidents, incidence
infarction, infraction
infection, injection
inferior, anterior, interior
inpatient

kneecap
knuckle, nuchal
left-sided
lifelong
life-span
life-style
lightheadedness
long-standing
loop, loupe
loose, lose
low-grade fever
mealtime
mucous, mucus
mid-60s (pulse rate)
midback
midbrain
midline
midsection
midwife
multi-infection
multiview
nail bed
nearsightedness
necrosis, nephrosis, neurosis, narcosis
nevertheless
nighttime
nonimmune
noninvasive
nonmedical
non-neoplastic
nontender
nonunion
nonverbal
nose drops
nosebleed
ongoing
onset
outpatient
output
overbite
overhang
overshoot
overweight
pacemaker
painkiller

palpation, palpitation
passed, past
per se
perfusion, profusion
perineal, peritoneal, peroneal
perineum, peritoneum
piece, peace
plain, plane
postmortem
postpartum
posture, posterior
preeclampsia
preemployment
preoperative
preexisting
pursestring suture
radicle, radical
radiculitis, ridiculous
rale, rail
recession, resection
reflex, reflux
sac, sack
seat belt
sight, site, cite
slitlike
stationary, stationery
Steri-Strip
suppuration, separation
their, there, they're
through, thorough
time card
tinnitus, tendonitis
toenail
toothache
track, tract
twofold
tympanites, tympanitis
ultrasound
ureter, urethra
widespread
workout
workup (n.), work up (v.)
X ray (n.), X-ray (adj.)

APPENDIX D
ABBREVIATIONS

◆ ABBREVIATIONS FOR WEIGHTS AND MEASURES
(medication dosages and lab values)

length or thickness

centimeter	cm
meter	m
millimeter	mm

weight

grain	gr
gram	g or gm
kilogram	kg
milligram	mg
microgram	mcg

volume

cubic centimeter	cc
liter	L
milliliter	mL (liquid volume)

◆ ABBREVIATIONS DESIGNATING TIMES AND METHODS

a.c.	before meals
b.i.d. or BID	twice a day
h or H	hour
IM	intramuscular
IV	intravenous
NPO	nothing per os
p.c.	after meals
PO	per os (by mouth)
PRN	as desired or as needed
q or Q	every
q.i.d. or QID	four times a day
q2h or Q2H	every two hours
qd or QD	every day
qh or QH	every hour
qod or QOD	every other day
stat or STAT	immediately
subq/subcu	subcutaneous
t.i.d. or TID	three times a day

◆ ABBREVIATIONS RELATED TO CHART NOTES

BP	blood pressure
CC	chief complaint
ER	Emergency Room
FH	family history
F/U	follow-up
GI	gastrointestinal

GU	genitourinary
GYN	gynecology
H&P	history and physical
HPI	history of present illness
HS	hour of sleep
ICU	Intensive Care Unit
NPO	nothing per os (by mouth)
OB	obstetrics
PE	physical exam
PERRLA	pupils equal, round, reactive to light and accommodation
PMH	past medical history
PRN	as necessary or as desired
R/O	rule out
ROS	review of systems
SH	social history
S/P	status post
STAT or stat	right now
TPR	temperature, pulse, respirations
UA	urinalysis
VS	vital signs

Brief forms (short forms) are accepted forms of full words that are not abbreviated. Generally, they are derived from common usage. Some examples are listed here:

chem profile	chemistry profile
cysto	cystoscopy
echo	echocardiogram
exam	examination
flex sig	flexible sigmoidoscopy
flu	influenza
Pap smear	Papanicolaou smear
pro time	prothrombin time
rehab	rehabilitation
sed rate	sedimentation rate
temp	temperature

APPENDIX E
LABORATORY TESTS

ALKALINE PHOSPHATASE (al´kă-lĭn fos´fă-tās)

Alkaline phosphatase (alk phos) is an enzyme found primarily in the liver and in bone. The test is useful in diagnosing and monitoring the progress of liver disease, medications that are toxic to the liver, and bone diseases.

Normal range: 20 to 90 IU/L

AMYLASE (am´il-ās)

Amylase is a digestive enzyme, produced in the pancreas, salivary glands, and liver. Normally very little amylase is found in the blood or urine. Serum levels are used to evaluate pancreatitis; urine amylase is performed on a 2-hour or 24-hour specimen.

Normal serum level: 60 to 160 Somogyl U/L

BILIRUBIN (bil-i-rū´bin)

Bilirubin is a pigmented by-product of hemoglobin breakdown, carried to the liver for further metabolism, and then excreted through the bile ducts into the intestine, giving the stool its normal brown color. It is called *indirect* before being acted on by the liver, and it is called *direct* after being metabolized by the liver. The *total bilirubin* combines both of these measurements; if this is abnormally high, then the individual determinations are made. Abnormalities in bilirubin level may be due to liver disease, infectious mononucleosis, gallbladder disease, or blood disease. It may be measured in serum or urine.

Normal serum level: direct, less than 0.3 mg/dl;
indirect, 0.1 to 1.0 mg/dl;
total bilirubin, 0.1 to 1.2 mg/dl (1 to 12 in newborns)

BUN (blood urea nitrogen)

Urea is an end product of protein breakdown. It is formed in the liver, found in the blood in the form of urea nitrogen, and excreted in the urine by the kidneys. BUN is a test for kidney function.

Normal value: 8 to 23 mg/dl

CHOLESTEROL (kō-les´ter-ol)

Cholesterol is a fatty substance (lipid) found in body tissue. It is an essential building block of cell membranes, bile acids, and sex hormones. High levels are associated with the development of coronary artery disease. Cholesterol attaches to proteins in complexes called *lipoproteins* and travels through the bloodstream. The LDL (low-density lipoprotein), or *bad cholesterol,* forms deposits in arterial walls. The HDL (high-density lipoprotein), or *good cholesterol,* may help protect people from coronary artery disease.

Average value is 150 to 200 mg% with the following:
HDL normal, less than 130;
LDL normal, greater than 60; and
total cholesterol to HDL ratio of 3.4

COMPLETE BLOOD COUNT (CBC)

This may include seven to eight different tests including the following:

HEMATOCRIT measures the portion of blood volume that is made up of red cells. It is commonly used to test for anemia.

Normal values: women, 37% to 47%; men, 40% to 54%

HEMOGLOBIN is the iron-containing protein found in the red blood cells that carries oxygen to the body tissues. It is a test for anemia.

Normal values: women, 12 to 16 gm/dl; men, 14 to 18 gm/dl

RED BLOOD CELL COUNT (RBC): These cells carry oxygen to body tissues, as well as waste products being returned to the lungs. This is also a test for anemia.

Normal values: women, 4.2 to 5.4 million/cu mm;
men, 4.6 to 6.2 million/cu mm

WHITE BLOOD COUNT (WBC) and **DIFFERENTIAL:** The white cells fight infection. Increases in WBCs indicate infection; decreases indicate loss of ability to fight infection.

There are several types of white cells, each with a specific function. They include *neutrophils* (PMNs or polys), *bands* (stabs), *lymphocytes* (lymphs), *monocytes* (monos), *eosinophils* (eos), and *basophils.*

Normal values: WBC, 4500 to 11,000; PMNs, 47% to 77%;
stabs, 0% to 3%; lymphs, 16% to 43%; monos, 0.5% to 10%;
eos, 0.3% to 7%; basophils, 0.3% to 2%

PLATELETS: These thrombocytes are important in blood clotting and may be evaluated before surgery to diagnose blood diseases, to assess chemotherapy, and to monitor some forms of drug therapy.

Normal values: 150,000 to 400,000

CREATININE   (krē-at´i-nēn)

Creatinine is a waste substance from the blood filtered by the kidneys and excreted in the urine. It can be measured in the blood or urine. It is a measurement of kidney function.

Normal serum creatinine: 0.6 to 1.2 mg/dl
Creatinine clearance (urine): women, 87 to 107;
men, 107 to 139 ml/minute

ELECTROLYTES (serum) (ē-lek′trō-lītz)

CHLORIDE is a mineral involved in water balance and acid-base balance of body fluids. Abnormalities may cause muscle spasms, breathing abnormalities, weakness, and even coma.

Normal value: 95 to 103 mEq/L

POTASSIUM is a mineral that helps maintain water balance in the cells and is necessary for electrical conduction in nerves and muscles, including the heart. Deficiencies may occur in diabetic acidosis, liver disease, severe burns, excessive use of diuretics, prolonged vomiting, and inadequate potassium intake.

Normal value: 3.8 to 5.0 mEq/L

SODIUM is involved in water balance, acid-base balance, and transmission of nerve impulses. Levels depend on the amount of salt and fluid in the diet, fluid losses, and various hormones. The kidneys play a role in excretion and maintenance of salt balance. Abnormalities occur as a result of dehydration, edema, and kidney disorders and may result in agitation, weakness, and confusion.

Normal value: 136 to 142 mEq/L

BICARBONATE (CO_2) is a buffer that keeps blood from becoming too acid. Much of the bicarbonate is formed through respiration, and the level is regulated by the kidneys. The levels are affected by severe vomiting or diarrhea, excessive intake of antacids, poisoning or other overdoses, diuretics, or difficulty in breathing. CO_2 levels are watched closely in disorders of the kidneys and the lungs.

Normal value: vary from 21 to 28 mEq/L

GLUCOSE (glu′kōs)

Glucose is the primary energy source for body tissues. It can be measured in serum or urine. The test may be used to diagnose hypoglycemia or hyperglycemia. (However, many factors interfere with the test.) This test measures the glucose at one particular moment.

Fasting blood sugar: 70 to 110 mg/dl
Two-hour postprandial blood sugar: 120 to 150 mg/dl

Glucose tolerance test (GTT) measures the body's response to a large dose of concentrated sugar over a period of several hours.

Glycohemoglobin (glycosylated hemoglobin or A1c) measures the percentage of hemoglobin molecules that have sugar molecules attached to them. This reflects the blood sugar levels over the preceding three to four months and is useful in indicating diabetic control.

Normal value: 3% to 6%

Accu-Chek is one method of checking the blood glucose level at home.

Clinistix is a test for excretion of sugar in the urine. The test paper should register negative; 1+ to 4+ indicates glucose is spilling into the urine and is frequently a finding in uncontrolled diabetes.

MONO TEST (heterophil test, mono spot test) (mon'ō)

Mononucleosis is a disease caused by the Epstein-Barr virus. There are two tests: The spot test is a screening test and is read as negative or positive. If positive, the heterophil test can be performed. A positive heterophil or one reported as a ratio greater than 1:224 suggests mononucleosis.

PROTHROMBIN TIME (pro time) (prō-throm'bin)

Prothrombin is one of a dozen factors necessary for blood clotting. This test measures the blood's ability to clot. An insufficient amount of prothrombin means it takes longer than normal time for the blood to clot. This may be caused by liver disease, bile duct problem, or medication. The test is performed to monitor oral anticoagulant therapy.

Values are given in seconds, normal (the control) being 11.0 to 12.5 seconds; when a person is on anticoagulant therapy, the value should be about $1^1/_2$ to 2 times greater than the control time. The INR is usually maintained around 2.

THYROID FUNCTION TESTS (thī'royd)

TSH is the thyroid-stimulating hormone. T3 and T4 are iodine-containing hormones. These tests are performed to evaluate thyroid function.

Normal values: T3, uptake 25% to 38%; T4, 5 to 11 mcg/dl;
TSH, 0.35 to 7 mU/L

TRANSAMINASE (trans-am'i-nās)

SGOT/AST (aspartate aminotransferase) is an enzyme found mainly in the liver and heart muscle and released into the bloodstream when either of these organs is damaged. The test may be useful in diagnosing and monitoring the progress of disease in either of these organs. Many drugs can cause liver injury, which results in an elevation of this enzyme.

Normal values: 10 to 40 IU/L

SGPT/ALT (alanine aminotransferase) is an enzyme found primarily in the liver and released into the bloodstream as a result of liver damage.

Normal value: 10 to 30 U/ml

URIC ACID (yūr'ik)

Uric acid is a by-product of body cell function as well as metabolism of certain foods. Uric acid may build up in the body in certain diseases such as gout and kidney disease. It may be measured in the blood or the urine.

Normal serum values: women, 2.7 to 7.3; men, 4 to 8.5 mg/dl

URINALYSIS (UA) (yū-ri-nal'i-sis)

The routine urinalysis (dipstick) gives information about nearly every organ in the body. It consists of a visual examination (color and clarity), which should be a pale or straw yellow and clear; specific gravity (concentration) 1.006 to 1.030; acidity (pH 4.6

to 8.0); chemical tests (glucose, ketones, protein, hemoglobin, bilirubin, and uro-bilinogen). Examination under the microscope indicates red cells, white cells, bacteria, casts, crystals, and miscellaneous substances if they are present.

THROAT CULTURE

Many organisms produce sore throats. The organism of most concern is the group A Beta-hemolytic streptococci (group A strep) because they can spread to the kidneys or to the heart valves. Cultures are "set up" for 24 hours and then read.

Rapid Strep test gives an immediate response as negative or positive, but if negative and clinical signs indicate a more severe infection, probably a culture will be done for definitive diagnosis.

HEART ATTACK ENZYMES

Testing of three enzymes (CPK, AST, LDH) may be useful in confirming a heart attack. These enzymes leak out of damaged muscle and cause an elevation in their amounts in the blood. They are frequently drawn on consecutive days (serially). These studies are performed when a heart attack is suspected and aids in that diagnosis.

ELECTROCARDIOGRAM

This is a graphic recording of electrical activity generated by the heart. It is useful in detecting rhythm, size, and position of heart chambers; muscle inflammation; and abnormalities in minerals that control the electrical activity. It is also used to monitor drugs that affect the heart and to check the function of artificial pacemakers. EKGs are taken at rest.

Ambulatory (Holter) monitoring records heart activity over a 24-hour period.

Exercise EKG (stress test, treadmill test, and exercise tolerance test). This EKG is taken while the patient walks on a treadmill.

Echocardiogram (cardiac echo) shows sound waves (echoes) that are used to evaluate the size, shape, and motion of the heart. It may be used to evaluate abnormal heart sounds, an enlarged heart, palpitations, or blood clots thought to be from the heart.

CARDIAC CATHETERIZATION AND CORONARY ANGIOGRAPHY

This test is used to determine the severity and location of blocked arteries of the heart. Angiography may be done on other vessels throughout the body.

APPENDIX F
MEDICAL RECORD

◆ THE MEDICAL RECORD

The physician may use any of a variety of systems to record the medical data of patients. The patient's *chart, record,* or *file* is the accumulation of all data pertaining to that patient and will include any of the following documents:

- ◆ History and physical examination.
- ◆ Chart notes made by the doctor or nurse.
- ◆ Laboratory and X-ray reports.
- ◆ Special procedure reports.
- ◆ Correspondence.
- ◆ Forms used for a specific purpose, such as an immunization record, developmental and growth records for children, preemployment physicals, preoperative physicals, disability reports, and burn or injury diagrams.

◆ CLINICAL DATA RECORD

There is an entry or a notation made each time the patient is seen in the office. Entries include the date of the visit and the name of the person who saw or examined the patient.

◆ NARRATIVE NOTES

The notation begins with a statement about why the patient is seeking the physician's advice. This reason for the visit may be stated as a symptom or sign and may be referred to as the *chief complaint (CC)* or *problem*.

A complete physical examination is very detailed and follows this specific format:

HISTORY OF PRESENT ILLNESS (HPI), HISTORY, or SUBJECTIVE is information given by the patient. This information includes symptoms, when they began, associated factors, and remedies tried.

PAST MEDICAL HISTORY (PMI) includes illnesses, injuries, and surgeries the patient may have had as well as any allergies to medications or to other substances.

FAMILY HISTORY (FH) consists of facts about the health of the patient's blood relatives that might be significant to the patient's condition.

SOCIAL HISTORY (SH) and **MARITAL HISTORY** are included if pertinent to the patient's treatment. It may include eating, drinking, and smoking habits, as well as occupation and interests of the patient.

REVIEW OF SYSTEMS (ROS) includes a review of each body system, with the physician asking specific questions about the functioning of each system.

OBJECTIVE or PHYSICAL EXAMINATION (PE) provides an examination record. Laboratory and X-ray findings are also considered objective information, although they are usually placed in a separate paragraph.

DIAGNOSIS, ASSESSMENT, IMPRESSION, APPRAISAL, or **CONCLUSION** provides the examining physician's interpretation of the information.

This may need further studying, in which case a diagnosis may be referred to as *rule out (R/O)*, and further studies will be planned.

PLAN, DISPOSITION, TREATMENT, RECOMMENDATIONS, or **ADVICE** include instructions to the patient, additional investigational procedures to be performed, medications prescribed, and so forth.

In *routine* physician office visits, referring to any visit other than a physical exam, the examination is limited to the immediate complaint or symptom. These visits may also be referred to as checkups, rechecks, or progress notes. (*Patient returns to recheck ears. Patient returns for blood pressure check.*)

The sequence of headings for a complete history and physical examination may include the following:

- ◆ CHIEF COMPLAINT
- ◆ HISTORY OF PRESENT ILLNESS
- ◆ PAST MEDICAL HISTORY
- ◆ ALLERGIES
- ◆ MEDICATIONS
- ◆ SURGERIES
- ◆ FAMILY HISTORY
- ◆ SOCIAL HISTORY
- ◆ REVIEW OF SYSTEMS
- ◆ PHYSICAL EXAMINATION
    - GENERAL
    - HEENT
    - NECK
    - CHEST
    - LUNGS
    - HEART
    - ABDOMEN
    - PELVIC
    - RECTAL
    - EXTREMITIES
    - NEUROLOGIC
- ◆ IMPRESSION
- ◆ PLAN

APPENDIX G
AAMT JOB DESCRIPTION

The American Association for Medical Transcription (AAMT) represents the medical transcription profession. AAMT has created a model job description, which is a practical, useful compilation of the basic job responsibilities of a medical transcriptionist.

AAMT defines a medical transcriptionist as a medical language specialist who interprets and transcribes dictation by physicians and other health care professionals regarding patient assessment, workup, therapeutic procedures, clinical course, diagnosis, prognosis, etc., in order to document patient care and facilitate delivery of health care services.

◆ AAMT MODEL JOB DESCRIPTION

Knowledge, Skills, and Abilities

1. Minimum education level of associate degree or its equivalent in work experience and continuing education.
2. Knowledge of medical terminology, anatomy and physiology, clinical medicine, surgery, diagnostic tests, radiology, pathology, pharmacology, and the various medical specialties as required in areas of responsibility.
3. Knowledge of medical transcription guidelines and practices.
4. Excellent written and oral communication skills, including English usage, grammar, punctuation, and style.
5. Ability to understand diverse accents and dialects and varying dictation styles.
6. Ability to use designated reference materials.
7. Ability to operate designated word processing, dictation, and transcription equipment, and other equipment as specified.
8. Ability to work independently with minimal supervision.
9. Ability to work under pressure with time constraints.
10. Ability to concentrate.
11. Excellent listening skills.
12. Excellent eye, hand, and auditory coordination.
13. Certified medical transcriptionist (CMT) status preferred.

Working Conditions

General office environment. Quiet surroundings. Adequate lighting.

Physical Demands

Primarily sedentary work with continuous use of earphones, keyboard, foot control, and, where applicable, video display terminal.

Job Responsibilities

1. Transcribes medical dictation to provide a permanent record of patient care.
2. Demonstrates an understanding of the medicolegal implications and responsibili-

ties related to the transcription of patient records to protect the patient and the business/institution.

3. Operates designated word processing, dictation, and transcription equipment as directed to complete assignments.

4. Follows policies and procedures to contribute to the efficiency of the medical transcription department.

5. Expands job-related knowledge and skills to improve performance and adjust to change.

6. Uses interpersonal skills effectively to build and maintain cooperative working relationships.

Performance Standards

1.1	Applies knowledge of medical terminology, anatomy and physiology, and English language rules to the transcription and proofreading of medical dictation from originators with various accents, dialects, and dictation styles.
1.2.	Recognizes, interprets, and evaluates inconsistencies, discrepancies, and inaccuracies in medical dictation, and appropriately edits, revises, and clarifies them without altering the meaning of the dictation or changing the dictator's style.
1.3	Clarifies dictation that is unclear or incomplete, seeking assistance as necessary.
1.4	Flags reports requiring the attention of the supervisor or dictator.
1.5	Uses reference materials appropriately and efficiently to facilitate the accuracy, clarity, and completeness of reports.
1.6	Meets quality and productivity standards and deadlines established by employer.
1.7	Verifies patient information for accuracy and completeness.
1.8	Formats reports according to established guidelines.
2.1	Understands and complies with policies and procedures related to medicolegal matters, including confidentiality, amendment of medical records, release of information, patients' rights, medical records as legal evidence, informed consent, etc.
2.2	Meets standards of professional and ethical conduct.
2.3	Recognizes and reports unusual circumstances and/or information with possible risk factors to appropriate risk management personnel.
2.4	Recognizes and reports problems, errors, and discrepancies in dictation and patient records to appropriate manager.
2.5	Consults appropriate personnel regarding dictation that may be regarded as unprofessional, frivolous, insulting, inflammatory, or inappropriate.
3.1	Uses designated equipment effectively, skillfully, and efficiently.
3.2	Maintains equipment and work area as directed.
3.3	Assesses condition of equipment and furnishings, and reports need for replacement or repair.
4.1	Demonstrates an understanding of policies, procedures, and priorities, seeking clarification as needed.
4.2	Reports to work on time, as scheduled, and is dependable and cooperative.
4.3	Organizes and prioritizes assigned work, and schedules time to accommodate work demands, turnaround-time requirements, and commitments.
4.4	Maintains required records, providing reports as scheduled and upon request.
4.5	Participates in quality assurance programs.
4.6	Participates in evaluation and selection of equipment and furnishings.
4.7	Provides administrative/clerical/technical support as needed and as assigned.
5.1	Participates in inservice and continuing education activities.
5.2	Provide documentation of inservice and continuing education activities.
5.3	Reviews trends and developments in medicine, English usage, technology, and transcription practices, and shares knowledge with colleagues.

5.4   Documents new and revised terminology, definitions, styles, and practices for reference and application.

5.5   Participates in the evaluation and selection of books, publications, and other reference materials.

6.1   Works and communicates in a positive and cooperative manner with management and supervisory staff, medical staff, co-workers and other health care personnel, and with patients and their families when providing information and services, seeking assistance and clarification, and resolving problems.

6.2   Contributes to team efforts.

6.3   Carries out assignments responsibly.

6.4   Participates in a positive and cooperative manner during staff meetings.

6.5   Handles difficult and sensitive situations tactfully.

6.6   Responds well to supervision.

6.7   Shares information with co-workers.

6.8   Assists with training of new employees as needed.

APPENDIX H
AAMT CODE OF ETHICS

◆ PART I ASSOCIATION MEMBERSHIP

Preamble
Be aware that it is by our standards of conduct and professionalism that the American Association for Medical Transcription (AAMT) is evaluated. As members of AAMT we should recognize and observe the goals and objectives of the organization and the limitations and confinements imposed by its bylaws, policies, and procedures.

Scope of Member Conduct
AAMT members (in individual categories of membership) will:
1. Place the goals and purposes of the Association above personal gain and work for the good of the profession.
2. Discharge honorably and to the best of their ability the responsibility of any elected or appointed Association position.
3. Preserve the confidential nature of professional judgments and determinations made confidentially by the official bodies of the Association.
4. Represent truthfully and accurately (a) one's membership in the Association, (b) one's roles and functions in the Association, and (c)any positions and decisions of the Association.

◆ PART II PROFESSIONAL STANDARDS

Preamble
AAMT members are aware that it is by our standards of conduct and professionalism that the entire profession of medical transcription is evaluated. We should conduct ourselves in the practice of our profession so as to bring dignity and honor to ourselves and to the profession of medical transcription as medical language specialists. Therefore, the following standards are considered essential in the workplace:
1. A medical transcriptionist undertakes work only if s/he is competent to perform it.
2. A medical transcriptionist exhibits honesty and integrity in his/her professional work and activities.
3. A medical transcriptionist is reasonably familiar with and complies with principles of accuracy, authenticity, privacy, confidentiality, and security concerning patient care information.
4. A medical transcriptionist engages in professional reading and continuing education sufficient to stay abreast of important professional information.
5. A medical transcriptionist does not misrepresent or falsify information concerning medical records, his/her fees, work or professional experience, credentials, or affiliations.
6. A medical transcriptionist complies with applicable law and professional standards governing his/her work.
7. A medical transcriptionist does not assist others to violate ethical principles or professional standards of the medical transcription field.
8. If a medical transcriptionist learns of a significant unethical practice by another medical transcriptionist, s/he takes reasonable steps to resolve the matter.
9. A medical transcriptionist who agrees to serve in an official capacity in a professional association exhibits honesty and integrity in discharging his/her responsibilities.
10. AAMT members who are not medical transcriptionists should abide by the above principles where applicable.

Reprinted by permission. © 1995 American Association for Medical Transcription, PO Box 576187, Modesto, CA 95357-6187.